ENGLISH LANGUAGE ARTS
AND READING ON THE INTERNET

ENGLISH LANGUAGE ARTS AND READING ON THE INTERNET

A Resource for K–12 Teachers

Second Edition

James C. Greenlaw
Saint Francis Xavier University

Jazlin V. Ebenezer, Series Editor
Wayne State University

Upper Saddle River, New Jersey
Columbus, Ohio

Library of Congress Cataloging in Publication Data

Greenlaw, Jim, 1952–
    English language arts and reading on the Internet: a resource for K–12 teachers/James C. Greenlaw:
Jazlin V. Ebenzer, editor—2nd ed.
        p. cm.
    Includes bibliographical references.
    ISBN 0-13-117589-0
        1. Language arts—Computer-assisted instruction.   2. Reading—Computer-assisted instruction.
    3. Internet in education—Directories.   I. Ebenezer, Jazlin V.   II. Title.

LB1576.7.G74 2005
428′.078′54678—dc22

                                                                                    2004044519

Vice President and Executive Publisher: Jeffery W. Johnston
Editor: Linda Ashe Montgomery
Editorial Assistant: Laura Weaver
Production Editor: Mary M. Irvin
Production Coordination: Karen Fortgang, bookworks
Design Coordinator: Diane C. Lorenzo
Cover Designer: Jason Moore
Cover Image: Corbis
Production Manager: Pamela D. Bennett
Director of Marketing: Ann Castel Davis
Marketing Manager: Darcy Betts Prybella
Marketing Coordinator: Tyra Poole

This book was set in Minion by Pine Tree Composition. It was printed and bound by R. R. Donnelley
& Sons Company. The cover was printed by Coral Graphic Services, Inc.

Pearson Education Ltd.   Pearson Education Australia Pty. Limited
Pearson Education Singapore Pte. Ltd.   Pearson Education North Asia Ltd.
Pearson Education Canada, Ltd.   Pearson Educación de Mexico, S.A. de C.V.
Pearson Education—Japan   Pearson Education Malaysia Pte. Ltd.

10   9   8   7   6   5   4   3   2   1
ISBN: 0-13-117589-0

For Ruth,

With love and thanks
for your patience and support

Preface

The purpose of this book is to introduce you to a selection of English language arts activities and resources that are available on the Internet's World Wide Web and to suggest ways in which you may most effectively make use of the websites examined in the text in order to transform your teaching of reading, writing, speaking, listening, and viewing. Because you may not have had much experience at using various search engines such as *Yahoo* and *Google* to find English teaching sites and materials on the Internet, our first chapter is devoted to explaining how such searches can be carried out. We also describe some of the electronic journals, professional organizations, and lesson plan sites that might be most fruitful. After this we describe the info-bar that will be used in Chapters 4 and 5 to summarize key features of the sites we are evaluating in terms of their intended audience, grade level, curricular fit, types of resources, site authorship, navigation, visual appeal, and interactive activities.

In Chapter 2 we discuss some of the recently developed theories about hypertextuality that form a necessary foundation for our explanation of the changes that technology is causing in K–12 language arts classrooms. To illustrate in concrete terms how these theories apply to actual teaching situations, we provide you with nine models of effective and imaginative uses of the Internet to teach language arts to your students.

In the third chapter we focus on recent research in the teaching of reading. We survey a variety of sites that offer you and your students excellent reading materials and lessons. Chapter 4 enables you to identify at a glance the strengths and weaknesses of many literature sites. In this chapter we review, for example, sites that contain information and activities intended to make the study of children's literature, young adult literature, mythology, poetry, short stories, novels, and drama more interesting and enjoyable for your students.

Finally, in Chapter 5, we examine the standards of the National Council of Teachers of English and the International Reading Association for evaluating student learning in K–12 English language arts courses. Then we explain how a variety of Internet sites can help you to enable your students to develop their knowledge of literature and their understanding of the writing process. These websites can assist your students in their attempts to research the history of English literature, receive constructive criticism from writers in electronic residence, take part in online grammar activities, write for newspapers and magazines, write speeches and e-mail, study English as a second language, compare English to other languages, and develop critical media literacy skills for studying newspapers and magazines.

At the end of each chapter, so that you can more fully appreciate the power of the sites that we include, we have listed a number of activities for you to try. As well, at the end of the book, we provide an Internet glossary for easy browsing.

Our primary goal in writing this book is to familiarize you with as many useful websites and teaching strategies as possible. While guiding you through the many fascinating texts and activities that these sites have to offer, we hope at the same time to engage you in a conversation about the nature of knowledge construction in cyberspace so that you can reflect upon what is worthwhile and rewarding for you and your students in the study of English language arts on the Internet.

We would like to thank the reviewers of this text for their insights and comments: Cathy Block, Texas Christian University; Ward A. Cockrum, Northern Arizona University; Claudia Cornett, Wittenberg University; Patricia P. Fritchie, Troy State University–Dothan; and Leanna Manna, Villa Maria College.

Contents

Glossary

Note: Every effort has been made to provide accurate and current Internet information in this book. However, the Internet and information posted on it are constantly changing, so it is inevitable that some of the Internet addresses listed in this textbook will change.

CHAPTER 1

Untangling the Web

- The Significance of the Internet for Teachers
- Browsing Through the Internet
- Sites for Internet Guides and Tutorials
- Resources for Reading and Language Arts Teachers
- Criteria for Evaluating Materials

THE SIGNIFICANCE OF THE INTERNET FOR TEACHERS

Whether you are a student teacher learning about the complexities of language arts pedagogy for the first time, or an experienced English educator interested in adding technological teaching components, you will find many useful and fascinating Internet sites that have mainly been developed by educators such as yourself. Perhaps you would like to download information about how to use puppets with your kindergarten students, or you hope to find music from India and Japan to add to your grade 3 integrated multicultural theme unit. You might wish to discover audio clips of Robert Frost's poetry for your grade 7 students to use in their multimedia anthologies, or video clips of actors performing Shakespeare for your grade 10 drama class. Then again, you may want to make a virtual visit online with the teachers of schools in Australia, South Africa, and Hong Kong in order to connect their students with yours to conduct intercultural collaborative writing projects together.

Your students' parents, the technology coordinators at your local district school board office, the government department of education computer consultants, and, of course, your students now all expect you to follow language arts curriculum guide objectives that stress technological competence as a basic literacy skill at the beginning of the twenty-first century. You have probably used a browser such as Internet Explorer to look up books on Amazon.com, and it is likely that before reading this book you have written e-mail to friends both in the country and around the world. Perhaps you have even done some serious web page construction and searched for lesson plans to use with your students. Regardless of your background knowledge, you will find the resources in this book to be helpful to you in your important job as a literacy worker.

If you were teaching language arts just a few years ago, you probably considered yourself lucky to be able to bring your class into a computer lab once a week to involve them in some basic word processing activities. If you did have access to the Internet, you may have found some information that was interesting to you personally but not of much value to you as a teacher. Yet now, you are probably expected to give your students regular and frequent assignments on computers. You have found so many sites on the Internet that are useful to you as a reading teacher that you could spend 24 hours a day trying to visit them all and hardly scratch the surface. Given the rapid rate of change in this field, it is difficult to imagine what technocultural trends and literacy lessons will be a part of teachers' lives a decade from now. But there is no doubt that for years to come language arts teachers will continue to be indispensable in helping disabled and gifted, English-as-a-second-language (ESL) and cultural minority students to read and write texts, and technological understanding is sure to continue as a significant factor in English educators' lives.

This first chapter provides basic information about the Internet before moving on to the contents of language arts and reading sites. If you are quite an expert at finding your way around the World Wide Web but have not had the opportunity to spend time looking for good sites to use in your teaching, then proceed now to the second half of this chapter to read about Internet resources for reading and language arts teachers.

BROWSING THROUGH THE INTERNET

The Internet is a huge network of interconnected computer networks linking the whole world. For example, the computers in a college of education can be linked to form a network of computers. This is what is known as a *LAN (local area network)*. This single network of computers is connected to other colleges in the same university, and the university computer network is then connected to a series of networks in other universities, school networks, commercial and business networks, government networks, industry networks, and many other networks throughout the world that transcend geographical barriers. All the computer networks have multilevel connections with telephones and satellites. Intercontinental telephone and fiberoptic connection lines run beneath the ocean floor to link all the continents.

An increasing number of websites are added each day to the Internet, making it more and more difficult to find relevant information. The emergence of search engines and search directories, however, has harnessed the overflow of websites. With definitive subject and topic *keywords* (words used by the search engines), information and resources on the Internet can be more quickly located and extracted. The Netscape and Internet Explorer browsers and search engines such as Yahoo and Google make finding information relatively easy for teachers who have mastered the necessary search strategies.

Each computer on the Internet is tagged, or personalized, with a set of numbers or letters known as the *IP (Internet Protocol) address*. The IP address enables you to search, locate, and connect to a specific computer that provides the information for which you are looking. To find a website on the Internet, a particular *syntax*, or arrangement of information, must be used to reach the "address" of the other computer. This Internet website address is called a *URL*, which stands for *Uniform Resource Locator*. An example of a URL for a website is

http://scils.rutgers.edu/~kvander/

The standard format for a URL is **protocol://host.domain/path**, in which

- The *protocol* is http (HyperText Transport Protocol) for an http type of information server.
- The *host.domain* is a reference to the server (scils.rutgers.edu).
- The *path* is a reference to the website on the server(/~kvander/).

This standard format, or syntax, allows the browser client software to recognize and to make the appropriate connections to the location of the websites. It operates in a manner somewhat similar to telephone or postal codes.

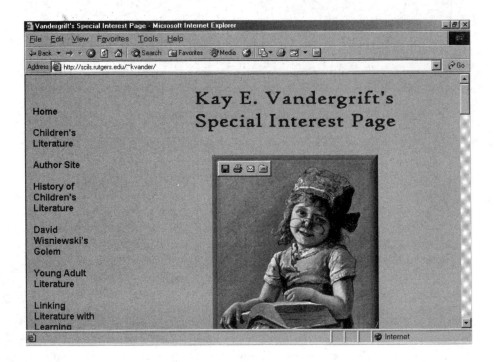

Most language arts teachers are familiar with how to conduct a basic Internet search with the Netscape browser, so this chapter will simply provide a few suggestions to make searches more fruitful. Traditional search engines (that is, engines that have been operating for more than a few years), such as *Yahoo* and *Google,* contain links to millions of sites for many of the terms that you might enter. For instance, when we recently typed in the search term "children's literature" on *Google* we encountered 2,570,000 "hits," or site references containing these words. By the time you read this book the number of sites will undoubtedly have grown. But when we used the Education K–12 menu on Yahoo and chose the category of *Children's Reading Lists,* we discovered a short collection of 12 reasonably useful sites. Our point here is simple. There is already far more information on the Internet about teaching language arts than anyone could ever possibly use, and much of it is not worth reading. Moreover, what is good is often difficult to find. So you need to develop strategies for narrowing your searches. Look for menus like those under the *Reading* category in *Yahoo.* Once you have found a good site (such as the ones listed in the following pages of this book), often it is linked to other sites that may be of interest to you and your students. Also, instead of entering broad search terms such as "children's literature," try to be more specific by using the name of an author, "Beverly Cleary"; a book, "The Cat in the Hat"; or a teaching method, "Creative Drama," and you are more likely to find shorter lists of sites that may be of use to you.

SITES FOR INTERNET GUIDES AND TUTORIALS

Guides and tutorials that will assist you in browsing through the Internet can be obtained at the following URLs.

Introduction to the Internet

For an excellent collection of guides and tutorials that are available on the Internet, see

http://www.december.com/web/text/index.html

Internet 101

The following website provides the basics on using the Net and includes tips on searching, e-mail, newsgroups, and chat rooms.

http://www.internet101.org/

Internet Explorer's Homepage

At Microsoft's Internet Explorer homepage, you can download the newest version of this browser. You can also learn how to stop pop-up ads and to customize your browser's appearance.

http://www.microsoft.com/windows/ie/default.asp

Jay Barker's Online Connection

To compare the major U.S. Internet service providers based on their speed, price, software, features, and support, see

http://www.barkers.org/online/

Netscape's Homepage

At Netscape's homepage, you can download Netscape's newest browser. You can also access a wide range of resources at this site.

http://home.netscape.com/

The HelpWeb: A Guide to Getting Started on the Internet

For helpful articles on how to navigate the Web, deal with e-mail spam, and many other important topics, see

http://www.imagescape.com/helpweb/welcome.html

RESOURCES FOR READING AND LANGUAGE ARTS TEACHERS

The following is just a brief sampling of some of the many sites that, because they attempt to provide K–12 English teachers with access to a wide variety of resources, are good places for you to begin your search for interesting language arts materials, resources, lesson plans, and professional information. As you navigate through these sites looking for other linked sites that may be useful to you and your students, you can keep track of those sites that interest you by clicking on the Bookmark button in Netscape or the Favorites button on Internet Explorer. *Bookmarking* enables you to keep a list of favorite sites. Then, the next time you wish to visit these sites, you simply open your list of bookmarks or favorites and click on the name of the site you want. The browser will take you right there. The first few sites described here contain literally hundreds of carefully organized links to language arts resources worldwide.

Clearinghouse on Reading, English, & Communication

http://www.indiana.edu

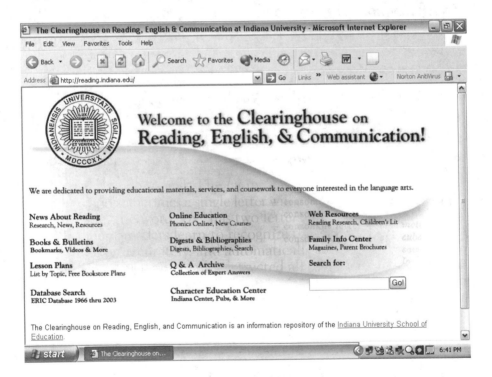

The *Clearinghouse on Reading, English, & Communication* provides a wealth of links to lesson plans, bibliographies, and Web resources as well as *listservs* on which you can learn more about elementary and secondary language arts by corresponding via e-mail with fellow English teachers. In its Web Resources section you can find links to a number of excellent sites that we describe in Chapter 3, such as *Tales of Wonder* and *The Children's Literature Web Guide.* You can also find sites concerned with *Theater and Drama, Journalism, Poetry, Storytelling,* and *Book Reviews,* to name just a few categories.

ISLMC Children's Literature and Language Arts Resources

http://falcon.jmu.edu/~ramseyil/childlit.htm

The Internet School Library Media Center (ISLMC) has developed a site called the *Children's Literature and Language Arts Resources* page that contains links to a wonderful assortment of children's literature sites, chat rooms, keypal organizations, curriculum resources, and enrichment activities. Among the noteworthy links from this site are *Young Adult Literature, Children's and YA Book/Media Awards, Authors and Illustrators, Biography/Autobiography, Multicultural Education Resources, Nonfiction, Picture Books, Series Books, Bibliotherapy, Families in Children's Literature, Spirituality in Kids' Books, Curriculum Units, ESL, Gifted Education, Literacy, Teaching Reading, Creative Dramatics,* and *Music and Songs.* Through each of these links you will have access to hundreds of excellent sites such as *KidsCom, Author Biographies for Middle and Secondary Students, Internet Research Project Student Resources, Multicultural Book Reviews, Historical Fiction Bibliographies,* and *The On-Line Visual Literacy Project.*

The English Server

http://eserver.org/

Another very interesting and useful place for you to consider as a starting point in your explorations of English sites is *The English Server.* This site was created by the English Department of Carnegie Mellon University for university English students and professors, but many of the sites to which this server is linked are of great value to elementary and secondary school English teachers as well. For instance, in its *Fiction* section you can find electronic versions of works by and about such novelists as the Brontës, Dickens, Defoe, and Conrad. The works of poets, dramatists, and journalists are also available in electronic texts. Related categories within this site include *Cultural Theory, Film and Television, Feminism, Art and Architecture,* and *Community Literacy.*

NCTE National Council of Teachers of English

http://www.ncte.org/

The *National Council of Teachers of English (NCTE)* homepage contains a wealth of information about English teaching ideas, standards, journals, jobs, research, teacher preparation, professional development, and discussion lists. If you want to order NCTE books on assessment, literacy, whole language, reading, and computers and technology, you will find their paragraph descriptions of these texts helpful. Some of the journals that can be ordered through this site are *English Education, Primary Voices K–6, Voices from the Middle, Research in the Teaching of English, English Journal,* and *Language Arts.*

The Internet TESL Journal

http://iteslj.org/

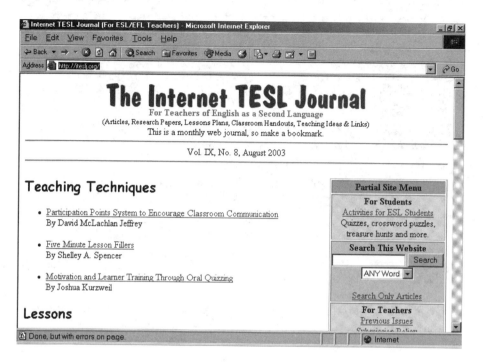

The Internet TESL Journal is a monthly publication that has been available on the World Wide Web since 1995. Because you can access back issues of this journal, you may download an amazing assortment of lessons and teaching ideas from this site. Or you can use the journal's own search engine to view many other ESL sites on the Internet. You can also read numerous articles and research papers, or you can view a variety of projects under such headings as conversation questions, jokes, games, and activities. This site is an essential starting point for teachers and students of ESL and EFL.

Reading Online

http://www.readingonline.org/

Reading Online is an electronic journal of the International Reading Association. Its contributors include K–12 reading teachers and teacher educators. The articles are nicely organized in *hypertext* format so that you can, for example, click on the title of a book being discussed by the article's author and move immediately to a description of that book on a database such as the *Clearinghouse on Reading, English, & Communication*. After you finish reading the article, you are encouraged by the

A screen shot of *http://www.readingonline.org*. Reprinted with permission of the International Reading Association. All rights reserved.

journal's editors to take part in an online discussion forum about the issues it raises. In the *International Perspectives* section of the journal you can read, for example, an article about research on literacy in Malaysia, and in the *Electronic Classroom* section you can read an article titled "Technology and the Revival of the Hawaiian Language."

CRITERIA FOR EVALUATING MATERIALS

Web-searching tools such as *Netscape* and *Internet Explorer* have made searching and publishing on the Internet very easy. New websites are continually being added. At present there are an estimated 280 million English native speakers using the Internet and another 680 million non-English speakers on the Internet (*Global Internet Statistics,* **http://www.glreach.com/globstats/**).

Many search engines are available, but we found *Google* and *Yahoo* to be the most important for English education. For every hit with each search engine, there are thousands of sites on a given topic of research, making it impossible to go through all the sites. In writing this book we visited many sites and followed links to categories and subcategories. Although some sites sounded very exciting, when we opened them, the message was a disappointing, "File Not Found. . . . The requested

URL was not found on the server." Perhaps one out of every 20 websites proved "Networthy." Searching can be time-consuming and frustrating, and it requires considerable patience. You must overcome these obstacles to use the Internet meaningfully and help your students to do the same. The following is a list of criteria for the selection of resources on the Internet:

1. The lesson plan on the Internet should match the objectives and outcomes of your department of education's curriculum.
2. English content of an activity should be at the appropriate developmental level.
3. Reading level should be grade and age appropriate.
4. Meaningful information and activities for both teachers and students should be presented.
5. Lesson plans and activities should reflect critical thinking; constructivism; integration of reading, writing, speaking, listening, viewing, and representing; and multiple approaches to teaching and learning.
6. Links to other related websites should be provided.
7. Background information should be included with lesson plans.
8. Connections to experts, peers, teachers, or mailing lists should be provided.
9. Activities should be online or downloadable to local disks.
10. Information should be presented with a multimedia approach—sound, animation, and aesthetically pleasing graphics.
11. Articles and papers should include complete references.

We have explored many websites in language arts and reading education, and, based upon the preceding criteria, we have selected sites that are useful for both teachers and students. But you should also work your way through these sites before you recommend them to your students.

The Internet can be incorporated easily into English teaching and learning. It offers both practical information and activities and theoretical constructs to consider. It can also bring about a shift in power from you to your students.

In Chapters 3, 4, and 5 we have brought together an annotated collection of websites that provide a variety of resources for teaching reading and English language arts. Our intent is to offer you a broad sampling of the many Internet sites that contain resources for teaching English. The sites included in Chapter 3 focus on research and lesson plans for teachers of reading. Chapter 4 includes a multitude of sites about the kinds of literature and authors taught in K–12 classrooms. And the language arts sites we provide for you in Chapter 5 have been selected to correspond to the NCTE and IRA standards for English language arts that we present at the beginning of the chapter. The sites in Chapter 5 are organized into the following categories: English Language Arts Standards, Researching the History of the English Literature, Grammar Online, Publishing and Exploring Student Writing, Writing for

Newspapers and Magazines, Debating and Speech Writing, Composing and Sharing Multimedia Presentations, English as a Second Language (ESL) Projects and Resources, Intercultural Communication via E-mail, Comparing Other Languages with English, Creating School Homepages, and Newspapers and Magazines.

The assessment of the grade-level suitability of the resources contained at a site is best seen as an approximate guide for several reasons. The resources often can be applied to a number of grade levels. The authors of the sites sometimes state the intended grade level, but often they do not. State and provincial education authorities generally determine the grade-level suitability of concepts and skills included in curriculum documents. There is no universal agreement on these issues. And, of course, the readiness of students to learn must also be taken into account when determining grade-level suitability.

Useful information is provided for each listed site: its title and URL, a description of its pertinent features, and a profile consisting of eight components:

1. *Intended audience:* Teachers, teachers and students, or just students.
2. *Grade level:* One or more grades from K–12.
3. *Curricular fit:* For example, creative writing and drama in the English and theater arts class.
4. *Types of resources:* For example, links to various worthwhile ESL project sites.
5. *Authorship of site:* Commercial enterprise, university/school, government agency, professional organization, or private individual.
6. *Navigation:* Satisfactory, good, or very good.
7. *Visual appeal:* Satisfactory, good, or very good.
8. *Interactive activity:* For example, some opportunity to take part in discussion groups.

For most of the sites in Chapters 4 and 5 we have organized the preceding information in the following chart form:

http://	
Intended Audience	
Grade Level	
Curricular Fit	
Types of Resources	
Authorship of Site	
Navigation	
Visual Appeal	
Interactive Activity	

Intended audience refers to the audience (teachers, students, or both) who would benefit most from the material found at the site. *Grade level* refers to the recommended grade level or levels for the material found at the site. *Curricular fit* refers to the main English areas/topics that the site addresses (e.g., grammar, young adult literature, etc.). *Types of resources* refers to whether the site is a collection of links to other sites (a gateway site) or a storehouse of specific content (e.g., puppetry activities, E-text of British literature, etc.), or both. *Authorship of site* refers to the creator of the site (i.e., a private individual, a university, or some other type of organization). *Navigation* refers to how simple and convenient it is for the user to access various parts of the site.

Visual appeal refers to how well the site might capture the user's interest because of the way the site is organized and the extent to which graphics and special effects are used. Visual appeal likely has the most relevance for sites that are intended for students. It also provides a rough measure of the display speed of a site, because a site with very good visual appeal tends to be graphics-rich in the design of its web pages. This kind of site will have a slower display speed, while a site with minimal graphics will have a faster display speed.

Interactive activity refers to the extent of interaction that is possible between the user and the site's resources. The word "None" means that all the user can do is read and look at pictures or go to other links. If, on the other hand, students may leave copies of their writing at a site, become involved in discussion groups, listen to a famous poet reading his poetry, etc., then we usually describe in a phrase the pertinent activities.

SUGGESTED ACTIVITIES

1. Choose a search term such as "multicultural literature," "whole language," or "ESL," and compare the results with several different search engines such as *Yahoo* and *Google*.

2. Visit one of the professional organization sites listed in this chapter and subscribe to a teachers' newsgroup. After you read a sampling from the group's archives, submit a question to the group or contact one of the individuals who has raised an issue that interests you.

3. Visit the *ISLMC Children's Literature* or the *TESL* site, and follow its links to other related sites.

4. Use the criteria for evaluating websites that are provided in this chapter to assess the quality of some of the children's literature author sites listed on the *ISLMC* site.

5. Create two criteria of your own for evaluating Internet sites.

6. Consider a research question you would like to ask about reading, writing, student learning difficulties, etc., then visit the *Clearinghouse on Reading, English,*

& Communication site to search its research digests in order to see what some reading and language arts education experts have discovered thus far in answer to your question.

SUMMARY

We have described what the Internet is and have shown you how to find your way around the Internet. For detailed procedures on web navigation, we have referred you to a number of sites where guides and tutorials are available. In this chapter we have also introduced you to a few general English language arts sites. Our hope is that, with the assistance provided here, you will not become discouraged by the vast amount of information that you discover, but will use the helpful hints from this chapter to become an efficient and discerning Internet user. Happy browsing!

CHAPTER 2

English Education Reform in a Technological World

- Reform Through Technology
- Models for Internet Teaching
- Role of the Teacher
- K–12 Reading and Language Arts Sites

REFORM THROUGH TECHNOLOGY

Intellectual and communicative processes are integral to constructing and negotiating knowledge in the English language arts. Students need to be able to find evidence in texts to support their interpretations of literature. They must be able to generate their own questions about literature and propose possible answers. An English class should reflect the beginnings of the creative and critical aspects of literacy that the students will need to possess in their adult life.

In technologically rich societies such as the United States and Canada, *hypertextual reading* and writing skills and *lateral thinking* abilities are necessary components of literacy development. In his book, *Hypertext 2.0: The Convergence of Contemporary Critical Theory and Technology* (1997), George Landow suggests that hypertext's "emphasis upon the active, empowered reader, which fundamentally calls into question general assumptions about reading, writing, and texts, similarly calls into question our assumptions about the nature and institutions of literary education that so depend upon these texts" (p. 219).

Hypermedia and hypertextual sites on the Internet can provide wonderful opportunities for students to learn about the aesthetic features of literary texts. Through intercultural communication and through the exploration of cultural background materials, they can also learn from multiple perspectives about cultural representations of themselves and others.

Developments in cognitive and social psychology as well as technology in the last decade have provided new perspectives on learning. These new perspectives have contributed to the systemic reform of school curricula and ways of teaching and assessing instruction. Learning is presently viewed as personal, social, and situational. It also depends upon the attitudes, values, and interests of the learner. In line with these new developments, English education is focusing on lifelong learning and skill development that will enable students to inquire, construct new ideas, wrestle with complexity, cope with uncertainty and ambiguity, adapt to constant change, solve conventional and unconventional problems, and develop a high degree of interpersonal and intrapersonal competence.

Christopher Dede, a professor of information technology, argues that new technological developments can help transform schools if these developments are used to support new models of teaching and learning, models that characterize sustained, community-centered, constructivist classrooms for learner investigation, collaboration, and construction (O'Neil, 1995). The Internet can promote a collaborative culture in "doing English." For example, Jim Cummins and Dennis Sayers, in their book, *Brave New Schools: Challenging Cultural Literacy Through Global Learning Networks* (1995), have proposed that in order to avoid monocultural prescriptions for educational reform, teachers should establish "long-distance teaching partnerships across cultures, intercultural networks of partnerships that—to the greatest extent feasible—seek to take advantage of accessible and culturally appropriate educational and communications technology" (p. 11). In other words, they believe that teachers should use the Internet for intercultural communication if they want to (1) include such content and skills in their curricula as global education, literacy development, critical thinking, and second-language learning and (2) at the same time promote sensitivity to other cultural perspectives and to stimulate their students' research skill development. However, Cummins and Sayers also point out that, "as with any innovation in education—without an overarching conception of how to shape learning in the direction of the sort of critical inquiry that prepares our youth for the future, the global learning networks will merely lead to trivializing, superficial classroom practices that do little to reverse patterns of student, teacher, and community disempowerment" (p. 80).

MODELS FOR INTERNET TEACHING

In the past, teachers shaped children's conceptions about reading and writing literature and literary criticism by means of authorized, or prescribed, language arts textbooks. But the Internet has now become a major force in shaping young minds, and teachers who use Internet technology in their classrooms know the potential benefits it brings to the overall learning of their students.

How can you teach in a knowledge-intensive society? This is a challenge for most teachers—a reason we turn to computers and the Information Superhighway. When they graduate, young people are expected to be fluent in information literacy skills in the workplace. English education is the appropriate context for many of these skills to be developed. The online world enables children to explore a new set of experiences and helps them to satisfy their curiosity. Through experts' knowledge, the Internet can provide answers to questions that children ask.

What are the potential uses of the Internet in a language arts classroom? In the following section we present nine models to indicate just a few of the imaginative ways in which English teachers can expose their students to interactive learning experiences on the Internet.

Model 1: Collaborative Story Writing Across the Globe

In 1997 Deborah Falk, at Duck Bay School in Manitoba, posted the following project proposal on the Internet:

> I am looking to organize a story-writing project with interested schools. The way the project will work is that six schools will work together to write a story. When you register your class, I will form a Story Writing Group for you and five other classes. Each class will be assigned a one-week period in which to write their paragraph and email it to me during the assigned week. I will then send that paragraph to class two, who will write paragraph two, and so on . . . until the story is completed with paragraph 6. The reason that you will send the paragraph to me is so that I can forward the paragraph to all classes in your story group. I am combining geography with language arts.

Deborah also told the participating teachers in the project that there would be two groups of stories: those written for and by grade 1–4 students and those written by and for grade 5–8 students. After the stories were completed Deborah had enabled more than 250 students from the United States, Canada, Australia, and the United Kingdom to take part in the writing of 43 delightful stories.

Deborah's project demonstrated at least two of the virtues of a well-conceived Internet activity. The students had an opportunity to share their story ideas with other students around the world. They wrote with a group of international peers as their authentic audience. Also, they could see where their fellow writers lived on an online map of the world, so they learned about other countries as part of their assignment.

In another collaborative story writing project, grade 4 teachers Carla Churchulla of Maryland, Hanne Bentzen of Denmark, and Carolyn Brutan of South Africa, with the help of project facilitator, John Ost, enabled their students to collaborate on the Internet in order to write a multimedia novel titled *The Oil Spill Mystery*. You can read the novel and follow its links to related sites yourself by visiting the children's Kidlink project site at

http://www.kidlink.org/KIDPROJ/Kidwriters/Mystery/Maryland/index.html.

The teachers first heard about the project through an e-mail message on the Kidlink listserv. In order to coordinate their students' writing efforts they frequently had to send messages to each other using e-mail because of the time zone differences. The students in Denmark, for instance, were out of school before the Maryland students had awakened in the morning.

John Ost of New Hampshire met with the students online at least once a week to guide them in their writing. The classes created committees to handle different aspects of the project. They conducted regular committee meetings and wrote logs of their activities. The Writers Committee was in charge of adding ideas to the story once they had received input from all three classes. The Illustrator Committee was in charge of creating the illustrations for each scene of the story. The Mathematicians Committee created the math problems that were integrated into the story as it progressed. And the Researchers Committee carried out Internet searches to be sure that the facts of their story were true. For instance, they checked whether or not an eagle can fly across the ocean. They also checked out some facts about sea monsters. The Web Designers Committee learned how to create a web page and were responsible for designing the pages for their mystery. Finally, the Communicators Committee was responsible for writing e-mail messages to the students in the other two countries.

The resulting novel contained a really good, mysterious plot. The enthusiastically rendered illustrations were scanned into the computer and interspersed throughout the story. The web designers and researchers provided links to related sites on oil spills and sea monsters. As in the first case study discussed in this chapter (Deborah Falk's project), this one indicates some very creative thinking. E-mail communication, Internet research, web page design and construction, drawing and scanning of art work, and overall coordination of the group activities resulted in a rich and pleasurable learning experience for the participants. Furthermore, some delightful and instructive reading material was provided for other grade 4 students around the world.

Model 2: Reading Between Worlds—Intercultural Literary Interpretation

This project involved grade 10 Chinese-Canadian students in Vancouver communicating via e-mail with bilingual Japanese students in Kyoto to share their interpretations of a Japanese short story in English translation (Greenlaw, 1992). To begin the project the students were encouraged to become acquainted with each other through introductory messages. During these interchanges the students shared information about their schools and communities. For example, the Kyoto students pointed out that their school is located in the country, about 20 minutes from Kyoto Station, and that "Kyoto is one of the cities in Japan left with historical sites, such as famous temples and shrines that people from all over the world come to visit." They noted as well that they "enjoy shopping, talking with friends and other things" that their key pals would do in Vancouver.

During this introduction period the students were a little surprised, in fact, to discover how much they had in common with their key pals. For example, in Vancouver, Jennifer said, "I told [Masae] about my interests in acting and singing and it just happened that she was interested in the same things as me." While in the early stages it was beneficial for the students to establish a sense of common interests and concerns, as they came to know each other better, their pleasure in discussing cultural differences also grew.

At the same time that the students were becoming acquainted with each other through these personal exchanges, they also learned more about each other by sharing their interpretations of the short story, "Spring Storm" by Mori Yoko. Most of the students felt that this Japanese story provided a good starting point for their discussions about Japanese and North American culture. The story concerns a critical moment in the relationship between the actress Midori Natsuo and her husband, scriptwriter Asai Yusuke. On the day when Midori learns, much to her surprise, that she has been chosen to be the star of a musical, she also gradually comes to realize that her husband cannot accept her new career status because he feels it would diminish his own. As Mori Yoko's narrative unfolds, we see Midori's developing awareness of her predicament, first in her confused feelings of intense joy and suffocating pain while she approaches their apartment, then in her mistrust as she attempts to conceal the truth from Yusuke, and finally in her recognition of the choice that she must inevitably make between her marriage and her career.

In the following interchange with Jennifer concerning "Spring Storm," Masae's explanation of the meaning of the storm and blossoms indicated that she possessed a strong grasp of the theme of gender inequity as it was revealed to her through the story's symbolism:

> *This story probably got its title from the part where Midori and Yusuke talk about the storm and the cherry blossoms. When I read this story, I interpreted that the*

cherry blossoms were intended to symbolize women trying to "blossom" out into what was known up until then as the "men's world." The storm shows the men's discriminatory ideas against women, standing in their way and not letting them blossom. You can tell from what Yusuke says, that once the storm "stops," more women will be involved in the world. Midori's reply of how there will be more storms explains, in a way, that there will be more obstacles for women before they can really blossom.

At the end of the project the students in Kyoto and Vancouver each expressed their opinions about the process they had experienced. In Vancouver, Jennifer offered the following concluding remarks about "Spring Storm":

Masae said that Japanese culture was very much like it was in "Spring Storm." The women are supposed to stay at home. They're not supposed to go out into the business world because it's a man's world. She said that now they are starting to break away from that.

And, in Japan, Masae's remarks indicated that through her dialogue with Jennifer she had come to think about the story from an intercultural perspective:

In Japanese magazines for teens you read that guys hate girls who are smarter than them. In "Spring Storm" Usuke couldn't stand Midori earning more money than him. It's up to the individual person. I think our society has been stereotyped. My Dad helps out in the house now more than he used to. I wouldn't want to marry a guy who says that I have to stay at home and do housework. I'd probably give up working if I had a child, but, if not, I'd want to keep on working.

Model 3: Using Professional Writers and Senior Citizens as Mentors

There are many fine sites on the Internet devoted to teaching high school students how to write, but one of the most successful in terms of the opportunities it offers students to gain guidance from professional writers is the *Writers in Electronic Residence (WIER)* site (**http://www.wier.ca**). This site is located at York University in Toronto. Its founder was Trevor Owen. Over the past decade thousands of students have been aided in their writing by professional authors. The program has also facilitated the learning of writing skills by connecting students with teachers and with each other.

One significant aspect of WIER is Owen's recommendation that when students are working with their peers and mentors on their writing, all of their texts be printed out and stored in binders for further reflection to avoid the students focusing more on the technology than on the writing. Owen's point is an important one. Interactivity does not mean that students must remain glued to their computer screens as if they were playing a video game. They can certainly benefit by taking their peers' writing or their own work away from the computer to revise it in groups with pen in hand. In the same way, if they download an audio file of a speech or a piece of music, they can save it onto a CD to study at their own pace at home.

A variation on the WIER mentoring model could involve connecting K–6 students with senior citizens who would enjoy giving the youngsters the positive feedback they need to inspire them to write more stories, poems, and project reports.

Model 4: Sharing Your School Community with Others

Through the International WWW Schools Registry site (**http://www.grandpajunior .com/School-list.shtml**), it is possible to visit the homepages of thousands of schools around the world. When you do this you will discover that many of these schools have made efforts to introduce visitors to their staff members, students, and surrounding communities. If your school already has an active homepage, we recommend that you consider using it as a site for publishing your students' audio, photographic, and written essays and stories about themselves, their school, and their community.

Model 5: WebQuests

A *webquest* is a constructivist lesson that enables students to learn by exploring several sites in order to complete an assigned task. At the WebQuest site (**http:// webquest.org/**) you can follow helpful instructions for constructing your own webquests. This page contains a searchable database of activities, handouts, syllabi, PowerPoint slides, and other documents that can help you to learn how to develop and use webquests. Or you can introduce your students to some of the more than 500 ready-to-use English Language Arts WebQuests that have been developed by contributors to the site. A few examples of these projects include: (1) "Medieval Madness" in which time travelers are sent into the past to create a newspaper about the middle ages, (2) "Retelling the Classic Tales" in which students are responsible for all aspects of a performance of a play based on a fairy tale, (3) "Telling the Samurai's Tale" in which, while reading "The Samurai's Tale," students research Japanese culture, and (4) "Arthur Miller's 'The Crucible'" in which high school students research various persecutions of people throughout history and develop solutions to prevent such oppression from happening in the future.

Model 6: Researching and Constructing Thematic Multimedia Projects

One of the best ways that you and your students can make effective use of the Internet's unique power is to employ *multimedia* (sound and animation). Our suggestions in this model are primarily concerned with using the multimedia sites that other educators have created to make your students' Internet learning activities as hypertextually significant and attractive as possible. But we hope that after you encounter a few of these sites, you will be inspired to produce with your students your own multimedia Internet projects. The software and hardware that now exist for such productions are very user-friendly. If your school already possesses a few computers with an Internet connection, then the additional cost for items such as a basic image scanner should not prove excessive.

One well-conceived and imaginatively structured multimedia site that could inspire your students to carry out a thematic study of another culture as part of their reading, writing, viewing and listening activities is *Six Paths to China* (**http://www .kn.pacbell.com/wired/China/index.html**). Californian English language arts teacher Tom March created this site to illustrate to teachers how they might make the best use of the Internet in developing their own websites and hypertextual activities. As its title implies, this site contains six different approaches ("paths") to teaching students via the Internet about contemporary China.

In the first activity, called "China on the Net," March has collected a hotlist of resources from which teachers can derive their own student research projects if they wish. As part of a unit on Chinese and Chinese-American stories, for example, your students could, following March's first path to China, find sites on the arts, the environment, international relations, human rights, and many other topics.

March's second path, "Exploring China," encourages students to create their own multimedia scrapbooks in HTML (HyperText Markup Language) by developing a website of their own. Alternatively, they could employ other hypermedia software modes such as Hyperstudio to create a presentation from downloaded texts, images, video clips, and audio clips of China's places, cultures, and politics. The third path, "The Treasures of China," involves an Internet-based treasure hunt for information about China's past with which to answer questions about China's present situation, such as "What is China doing in Tibet that disturbs the Dalai Lama?"

In the final three activities March encourages students to examine their own feelings on issues. He asks them to carry out inquiry-based research and to conduct a role-playing activity. Each of his six approaches to studying various aspects of China is based on a wealth of World Wide Web resources both from within China and from sites around the world.

The special value of the *Six Paths to China* project as a source of English language arts activities lies in its ability to expose students to multimedia representations of China that have been carefully designed by the site's author to help students avoid simplistic, stereotypical conclusions about the Chinese people.

Model 7: Doing Author Studies

As you will see in Chapter 4, there is a vast selection of Internet sites regarding authors for children and adolescents. If your students are reading the works of Judy Blume, for instance, they can visit her homepage to learn more about her (**http:// www.judyblume.com/menu-main.html**). Blume provides young readers with information about her latest book and lists of other books by her that they might wish to read. She answers their frequently asked questions and provides biographical information and photographs of herself. We learn that Judy is founder and trustee of the Kids Fund, which is supported by royalties from several of her books, including *Letters to Judy,* a book of letters from her young readers. In her *Writing Tips* section she talks about writing "from the inside," keeping a trusty notebook, finding your own style, and rewriting. Judy emphasizes the importance of teachers being supportive of the creative writing attempts of students.

There are obviously many wonderful websites devoted to J. K. Rowling, the author of the Harry Potter books, but one that is designed especially with teachers and their young students in mind is the Scholastic "Kids Fun Online" site (**http://www.scholastic.com/harrypotter/author/**). Here your students may read the transcript of an extensive online interview between Rowling and many of her young fans in which the children ask the author questions such as, "How old is old in the wizarding world, and how old are Professors Dumbledore and McGonagall?" The *Scholastic* site also contains reference guides, a biography of Rowling, and a wonderful interactive game called the Wizard Challenge. The important points to remember when engaging your students in an author study activity are that the author sites should contain content that is at an appropriate reading level for the children and that there should be opportunities for the children to interact with the materials provided. This *Scholastic* site, for example, leaves readers young and old with the feeling that they have come to know J. K. Rowling better and that they have been able to learn something from her about the meaning of her books and the backgrounds of her characters. With luck, doing author studies will encourage your students to read more books by the same author.

Model 8: Researching Stories from Other Times and Places

This model for using the Internet to teach literature enables your students to make comparisons among a wide variety of cultures through their storytelling traditions. For K–6 students the site titled *Tales of Wonder: Folk and Fairy Tales from Around the World* at (**http://www.darsie.net/talesofwonder/**) contains a large and truly wonderful collection of tales including stories from countries such as China, England, India, Japan, and Russia as well as links to many more interesting folk and fairy tale sites. Students of all ages can enjoy comparing the themes and characters of these stories from different places. They will also notice, for instance, variations within countries such as the Tamil, Punjabi, Kashmiri, and Bengali cultures from which some of the Indian tales derive. To facilitate your students' understanding of these tales you might also involve them in research on the Internet into the features of the diverse cultures represented on this site.

Model 9: Having Fun with Media Literacy

In this model for using the Internet in your language arts program we wish to emphasize the pleasure that you and your students can experience in viewing and listening to media on the Internet and in producing your own video and audio presentations to share with others around the world. A good place to start when looking for worthwhile media literacy lesson plans is the University of Oregon's

Media Literacy Review site (**http://interact.uoregon.edu/MediaLit/mlr/home/ index.html**). Among the topics you will find there are advertising, critical viewing skills, news reporting, photo and visual arts, radio production, web page design, and script writing. One of the many sites to which *The Media Literacy Review* is connected through its Media Education Links is *CBC 4 Kids* (**http://www.cbc.ca/kids/ main.html**). Here, children in K–6 classes can listen to radio plays written and performed by grade 4 students. Then they can produce their own plays to submit to the CBC. Or they can take a virtual tour of the CBC Sound Effects Studio in Toronto to see how the radio technicians there produce the sounds of trains, the wind, marching feet, prison doors, and more.

For an excellent source of Canadian news and information shows, your students can visit the site titled *CBC On The Web* at (**http://www.cbc.ca/**). Here they may view transcripts of the television news show, *The National,* dating back to 1996, or they can download archived audio files of the radio programs. Transcripts are listed according to their date or subject. So if your students are doing research on "First Nations Issues" as part of a "Native Literature" unit and they want to view the text version of all of the news items referring to Aboriginal organizations, they can simply type in the words "First Nations" to find many stories that apply to their topic.

In all these models for using the Internet in your teaching, the students can grow in their knowledge of the world and themselves by collaborating on the Internet in reading, writing, speaking, listening, and viewing activities. The teacher in each case assumes the role of facilitator and guide of research and writing projects in which the walls of their classrooms dissolve, the distance between countries collapses, and students learn primarily from one another and from the materials that they find on the Internet. There are many other models for Internet use, some of which you will infer from the rest of this book, but the key point we wish to make here is that you need to rethink your role as a teacher when attempting to find or develop new curriculum approaches that involve the Internet.

ROLE OF THE TEACHER

Technology has greatly influenced the ways teachers teach and students learn. It puts teachers and students into a collaborative research mode. Students often teach themselves because they have in-depth knowledge about a topic as a result of their research via the Internet. This might be threatening to a traditional teacher because the power is shifted to the student. However, the responsibility of constructing knowledge must be rightfully returned to the learner!

With the use of the Internet's resources, teachers can put into practice Howard Gardner's theory of *multiple intelligences* very effectively, thus meeting the needs and interests of students. Students do not have to be locked into space, time, and resources. For example, Updegrove (1995) reports that in the Apple Classrooms of Tomorrow (ACOT) research project, in which high school students had many opportunities to use computers and networks to enhance their learning,

Students had significant growth in their independence and their ability to be collaborative problem solvers and communicators. . . . Teachers have shifted their educational approach from one of knowledge transfer (instructionism) to one of knowledge building (constructivism). Classroom instruction shifted from traditional lecture model to one that depended heavily on student collaboration and peer teaching (Apple Education Research Series, summary as cited in Updegrove, 1995).

Computers put the students in the ACOT project in contact with resources worldwide. The teacher's responsibility for stimulating students' interest in a subject still remains, which means guiding the students' thinking about a subject and challenging them to be creative in their approaches to analyzing the topic at hand. The teacher is a mentor and plays an interactive role with his or her students.

Internet resources allow English teachers to be highly creative in their teaching. Whereas students used to compare their ideas about literature with their peers in the same classroom, now they can share their interpretations of literature with students on the other side of the globe (Greenlaw, 1992).

K–12 READING AND LANGUAGE ARTS SITES

We include in this section a sampling of some of the ready-to-use interactive language arts units that are available for you on the Internet. Simply follow the instructions of the units' authors, and you will experience with your students just how enjoyable the Internet's language arts and reading sites can be.

SCORE K–12 English Language Arts Cyber Guides

The Schools of California Online Resources for Education (SCORE) site (**http://www.sdcoe.k12.ca.us/SCORE/cla.html**) is one of the best sources of such units. It contains approximately 140 web-based unit plans for grades K–3, 4–5, 6–8, and 9–12 English language arts teachers to use with their students. To give you a sense of the amazing variety of interactive activities that these units provide we will briefly describe four of them for you. These four units are based on Laura Ingalls Wilder's *Little House in the Big Woods,* Farley Mowat's *Owls in the Family,* Paul Zindel's *The Pigman,* and Aldous Huxley's *Brave New World.*

At the beginning of the grade 3 unit plan for Laura Ingalls Wilder's *Little House in the Big Woods,* students are shown images of cabins in the woods and asked to draw a picture of one of them and to write a description of what they see, using concrete sensory details. Then they are to read a description of wolves taken from the novel and view images of wolves in order to answer the question, "Why is the wolf the bad guy?" In the third activity the students are to read a number of recipes for maple sugar and then to write a maple sugar recipe of their own. The fourth activity involves students visiting an Internet site that features an authentic letter written by Laura Ingalls Wilder. After reading Laura's letter, students write a letter of their own to the children of the future telling them what life is like for a third grader in today's world. Finally, students are encouraged to read book reviews written by other students on the Internet and to then write their own reviews of the novel, *Little House in the Big Woods.*

The approach to teaching Farley Mowat's *Owls in the Family* to grade 4 or 5 students involves first of all guiding the students to sites on the weather and scenery of Saskatoon, Saskatchewan, in order for them to write a comparison between Saskatoon and their own hometown. Next the students are asked to conduct a virtual dissection of an owl pellet to determine what owls like to eat. Then, after visiting sites that contain images of the owl, they draw a picture of one of them. After writing and editing a friendly letter, the students are asked to visit two Farley Mowat author biography sites and to take notes on his life. They are then asked to make a list of things from Farley Mowat's life that appear in the book, *Owls in the Family.*

For Paul Zindel's *The Pigman* the authors of this web unit have included the following activities:

1. First, in order to be able to trace the excursions that John and Lorraine made with Mr. Pignatti, they make a map of New York City based on five different maps that they are directed to on the Internet.

2. Then they go on virtual visits to sites about the Guggenheim Museum, the Statue of Liberty, and Time Square.

3. Next they see slide shows of baboons and ceramic pigs and write an essay about the significance of these two symbols in the novel.

4. After this they send their teacher an electronic postcard in which they briefly describe their favorite setting in the story.

5. For the final activity, the students are asked to view a Venn diagram page to see how they can then create their own diagram to chart the similarities and differences among John, Lorraine, and Mr. Pignatti in three overlapping circles.

The five activities associated with Aldous Huxley's *Brave New World* involve students in writing four short essays and creating one simulation game by visiting pertinent sites on the Internet and doing research. The first essay, for instance, is on brainwashing, so the students carry out their research at sites on propaganda and advertising techniques. The other three essays deal with issues of cloning, legal constraints on people's freedom, and various social problems such as class warfare, mass culture, genetic ethics, and the dangers of Prozac. In the multimedia simulation activity, by using a free, downloadable multimedia authoring tool called Cocoa, the students create a world that illustrates the concept of conformity.

From this brief survey of just four of the many wonderful unit plans available at these language arts cyber guide sites, we hope that you now have a sense of the potential not only to make use of SCORE's teaching activities but also of how you might develop some of your own cyber guides in the future.

Doucette Index K–12 Literature-Based Teaching Ideas

http://www.educ.ucalgary.ca/litindex/

The *Doucette Index of Literature-Based Teaching Ideas* is a tremendous site, especially for teachers who are looking for print resources about commonly taught works of literature. The site contains a search engine that asks you to type in the title and/or author of a book you wish to teach. If, for example, you enter the title, *Julius Caesar*, into the search engine, you will find a list of five excellent, web-based teaching resources on the play and another six print-based teaching resources.

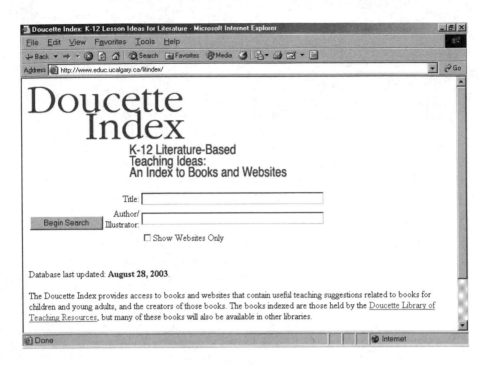

Blue Web'n: Blue Ribbon Learning Sites on the Web

The *Blue Web'n* page **http://www.kn.pacbell.com/wired/bluewebn/index.html** provides links to Internet sites containing (at the time of this writing) 8 tutorials, 118 activities, 15 projects, 43 lessons, 30 hotlists, 203 resources, and 23 references and tools for use by K–12 English language arts teachers and students. Here is a brief sampling of some of the descriptions of the valuable resources you will find at the *Blue Web'n* site.

Tutorials

■ *Writing Argumentative Essays.* Bill Daly, of the Victoria University of Technology (Australia), has provided a service to new writing teachers, high school students, and parents trying to help their children piece together an effective argumentative essay.

■ *The Shiki Haiku Salon.* This tutorial provides resources and a lesson in the poetic form of the haiku.

Activities

■ *Cyber English Syllaweb.* Here are some online English assignments that use technologies as tools and topics. The site, created by English teacher Ted Nellen, includes a booklist of literature with technology themes.

Projects

■ *Children's Express.* This is a news service produced by kids reporting on the issues that affect their lives.

Lessons

■ *Deep in the Bush, Where People Rarely Ever Go.* According to the *Blue Web'n* description of this site, teacher, Phillip Martin, collected these stories while he served as a Peace Corps volunteer in Liberia, West Africa. Included at this site is an extensive teacher lesson page, African recipes, links to other African resources, and ideas for your students to create and produce their own plays.

Hotlists

■ *Webtime Stories.* Replacing the *Kiddie Lit on the Net* site, this is an annotated hotlist of exceptional online stories, book and author resources, and online activites for people who love children's literature.

■ *Great Books Interdisciplinary Matrix.* Intended to support study of the "Great Books" championed by Mortimer Adler and Charles Van Doren, this site provides links to resources on 150 authors, many from the reading list for "How to Read a Book."

Resources

■ *Only a Matter of Opinion?* Editorials, columns, and editorial cartoons are classified as opinion pieces. This site encourages students to write and draw their own opinion pieces.

References and Tools

■ *Visual Thesaurus.* In this interesting way of exploring English language synonyms, words show up as a "spatial map of linguistic associations," with clickable words that encourage you to follow threads. The site uses Java and works best on newer systems.

■ *Biography.* A&E's *Biography* website includes a searchable and browsable online collection of 15,000 cross-referenced biographies from the *Cambridge Biographical Encyclopedia.* The site also provides selected opening chapters and reviews from best-selling biographies, a quiz, an anagram game, chatboards, and schedules of upcoming episodes of the *Biography* television program.

SUGGESTED ACTIVITIES

1. Using e-mail, contact teachers in two other schools. They can be teachers you know already in schools close to your own or teachers in schools in other states or countries. Arrange to have your students collaborate via e-mail in the writing of a group short story, novel, or poetry anthology.

2. Using e-mail, contact teachers in another country and plan to have your students collaborate with theirs in the interpretation of short stories, poems, novels, or plays. (Hint: It may be easiest to find common reading materials to study if you choose texts available on the Internet.)

3. Using e-mail, contact either some professional writers or, in the case of younger students, some senior citizens who might be willing to act as readers and editors of the creative writing your students produce. These mentoring relationships require some effort to set up, but they can be extremely rewarding for all involved.

4. With the help of parent volunteers, take your students out into the community with cameras and tape recorders with specific research plans in mind. Have them conduct interviews in order to paint a picture of your community on your school's homepage. The end result should help visitors to your school's website understand your community and it should also engender a sense of place and pride in your students.

5. Visit several webquests such as the ones described in Model 5. Once your study of these examples has given you a clear idea of how you would like to create a similar webquest yourself, think of a topic (My Journey to Mars, The Secrets of the King Tut's Tombs, Living in Medieval England, etc.) and then work with other teachers to find worthwhile sites to link to your webquest. Once you are satisfied that you have enough interesting sites for the students to visit in their quest, develop appropriate activities for them to carry out at each site. An interesting variation of this activity involves having your students compose a multimedia presentation of the experiences they encounter on their quest.

6. After studying Tom March's *Six Paths to China,* involve your students in creating their own "Six Paths" to India, Brazil, or Italy.

7. Have each of your students visit a website devoted to one of their favorite authors. Each student should be responsible for researching a different author, but all the authors can be writing in a particular genre (humor, adventure, science fiction, etc.) if you wish. After they have studied the site and read one of the authors' books, they can present a book talk and short author biography to the class.

8. Take your students to the *Tales of Wonder* site and have them carry out comparisons of two stories from different countries in order to discover common themes and archetypal patterns. Then encourage the students to write a similar tale set in their own culture. They may need to do further research on the Internet to learn more about the cultural backgrounds of each of the stories they are to interpret.

9. With your students, visit some of the many multimedia sites on the Internet and enjoy with them the activities available. If, for instance, you visit the *CBC 4 Kids* site, you could learn with the students how radio technicians generate various sound effects, then have the students create their own sound effects and write and record radio plays making use of these sounds.

10. Visit a number of the language arts interactive web units at the *SCORE* and *Blue Web'n* sites that are intended for students in the grade level(s) you teach. Select one of these units to share with your students.

SUMMARY

Clearly, a new paradigm for the teaching of reading and English language arts is emerging in which you need to be able to facilitate your students' learning on the Internet. Although the list of nine models for Internet use provided in this chapter is certainly not an exhaustive one, we hope that it has provided you with a sense of the possibilities that await you as you begin to consider your new role as a guide on the Information Superhighway.

REFERENCES

Cummins, J. and Sayers, D. (1995). *Brave new schools: Challenging cultural illiteracy through global learning networks.* New York: St. Martin's Press.

Greenlaw, J. C. (1992). Reading between worlds: Computer-mediated intercultural responses to Asian literature. *Reader: Essays in Reader-Oriented Theory, Criticism, and Pedagogy, 28,* 37–51.

Landow, G. (1997). *Hypertext 2.0: The convergence of contemporary critical theory and technology.* Baltimore: The Johns Hopkins Press.

Mori, Y. (1991). Spring storm. In S. Jeroski (Ed.), *Tapestries: Short stories from the Pacific Rim.* Scarborough, Ontario: Nelson Canada.

O'Neil, J. (1995). Technology and schools: A conversation with Chris Dede. *Educational Leadership,* October, 7–12.

Updegrove, K. H. (1995). *Teaching on the Internet.* **http://pobox.upenn.edu/~kimu/teaching.html**

CHAPTER 3

Reading Research and Lessons

- Teaching Reading
- Enabling Readers to Overcome Reading Disabilities
- Reading Recovery
- Adolescent Reluctant Readers
- Gifted Readers
- Fun with Words
- Storytime
- Lesson Plans for Teaching Reading
- Reading Across the Curriculum

TEACHING READING

Do you occasionally feel overwhelmed when you are faced with the task of teaching 30 students how to read? In a single class you may need to instruct children who are reading at various grade levels, some who are challenged by learning disabilities, and others who are gifted readers. You have been told by parents, principals, and professors that you must become aware of the many theories and methods of reading, such as whole language, reading recovery, and reading across the curriculum, but when you set out to make sense of these different pedagogical approaches, you discover that the field contains multiple, conflicting schools of thought. As will become clear in this chapter, the Internet can serve as a valuable resource for your work as a teacher of reading, whether your students are preschoolers or adults. In the following pages you will encounter brief summaries of articles and sites on the Internet that provide information about a wide range of issues and approaches from the field of reading research. You will also find a wonderful selection of reading lessons, enjoyable vocabulary activities, and storybooks on the web with which to entice your students into a lifetime of reading pleasure.

Learning to Read

http://toread.com/

The first site, titled *Learning to Read,* is the best place to start. The author, John Nemes, provides a clearly organized and comprehensive account of the reading process. He explains that there are basically three models of reading: (1) the *top-down models,* emphasizing what the reader brings to the text, such as prior knowledge and experiences; (2) the *bottom-up models,* emphasizing the written or printed text based on the idea that comprehension begins by processing the smallest linguistic unit (phonemes) first and then working toward the larger units (words, phrases, sentences); and (3) the *integrated models,* which recognize the interaction of bottom-up and top-down processes simultaneously throughout the reading process.

Among the topics discussed at the *Learning to Read* site are Using Cues for Reading Activities for Teaching Reading, What Are Literature Circles?, The Value of Free Reading, Book Discussions, Facts on the Teaching of Phonics, What Are Reading Skills?, Scaffolding and Modeling Strategies, Reading Comprehension Strategies, Teaching Word Identification, and Facts on Teaching Skills in Context. This site also contains an excellent collection of links to professional organizations, publications, authors, publishers, and interactive lessons. One of the many delightful interactive lessons, for instance, is a very rich unit for grade 1 children called *Teddy Bears.* This includes objectives, outcomes, activities, background information on teddy bears, stories, poems, assessment strategies, and lists of related books, videos and websites. The *Teddy Bear* unit has the potential to enchant beginning readers for many weeks.

After you have visited the *Learning to Read* site, you may wish to study some of the topics mentioned there in greater depth by examining the full text of the following reading research articles and books on the Internet.

The Reading Wars

http://www.theatlantic.com/issues/97nov/read.htm

Nicholas Lemann, the national correspondent for *The Atlantic Monthly* magazine, explores the political complexities of the battle between advocates of the whole-language and the phonics approaches to teaching reading. In his very entertaining and highly readable article, Lehmann concludes that "given that the traditional side is now winning the ongoing battle between traditional and progressive education, schools all over the country will be pressed hard by parents and politicians to move toward imparting skills and away from simply inculcating the joy of learning."

Sensationalism, Politics, and Literacy: What's Going On?

http://www.pdkintl.org/kappan/kfli9712.htm

In this PDK online article, Rona Flippo provides evidence that despite extreme differences in philosophy, expert reading researchers do agree on a number of practices and contexts with regard to reading instruction and development. These must not be ignored, she warns, in favor of what the politicians think.

Sixty Years of Reading Research—But Who's Listening?

http://www.pdkintl.org/kappan/kzem9903.htm

In another PDK online article, Steve Zemelman, Harvey Daniels, and Marilyn Bizar point out that 60 years of research and thousands of studies that resoundingly validate progressive approaches to literacy learning still have failed to produce the strong consensus we might expect. The authors explain why.

Whole Language and Phonics: Can They Work Together?

http://www.education-world.com/a_curr/curr029.shtml

In her *Education World* article, Sharon Cromwell argues that the majority of experts now contend that neither the whole-language nor the phonics approach by itself is effective all the time, but that both approaches possess merit. What does succeed then, many experts say, is a carefully designed reading program that employs part whole-language approach and part phonics, while taking into account each student's learning style and demonstrated strengths and weaknesses.

ENABLING READERS TO OVERCOME READING DISABILITIES

The Big "R"—Reading

http://www.ldonline.org/ld_indepth/reading/tutor_tips.html

This article offers some sobering facts about why good reading instruction is important. Up to 15 percent of children with reading problems drop out of school; only 2 percent finish college. Approximately 50 percent of teens and young adults with criminal records do not read well. About 50 percent of young people with substance abuse problems do not read well. About 90–95 percent of reading problems can be corrected with early intervention and appropriate instruction.

The following general advice is offered for reading teachers: When it comes to reading, directed practice makes perfect. Never force a child to read orally in front of peers. Choose reading material on subjects of interest to the child. Speak distinctly and expressively when reading, clearly enunciating words and sounds. Inflect your voice in accordance with punctuation. Help make reading enjoyable. Children with reading difficulties usually do not like to read and do not get sufficient practice to become fluent.

The remainder of the article provides valuable strategies for teaching students with reading disabilities such as dyslexia, speech and language disorders, processing deficits, and attention deficit/hyperactivity disorder (ADHD).

Academic Interventions for Children with Dyslexia

http://www.kidsource.com/kidsource/content2/dyslexia.html

This article, written by Julia Frost and Michael Emery for *KidSource Online,* suggests many types of interventions to help dyslexic children to learn to read. Here are just a few of them: Discuss the specific purposes and goals of each reading lesson. Teach children how metacognitive skills should be applied. Provide regular practice with reading materials that are contextually meaningful. Include many words that children can decode. Using books that contain many words that children cannot decode may lead to frustration and guessing, which is counterproductive. Teach for automaticity. As basic decoding skills are mastered, regularly expose children to decodable words so that these words become automatically accessible. As a core sight vocabulary is acquired, expose children to more irregular words to increase reading accuracy. Reading-while-listening and repeated reading are useful techniques for developing fluency. Teach for comprehension. Try introducing conceptually important vocabulary prior to initial reading and have children retell the story and answer questions regarding implicit and explicit content.

Preventing Reading Difficulties in Young Children

http://www.nap.edu/readingroom/books/prdyc/

This highly acclaimed study synthesizes the research on early reading development and makes practical, commonsense recommendations. The full 400-page text, edited by Catherine E. Snow, M. Susan Burns, and Peg Griffin for the National Research Council, is available here in HTML format. The study provides recommendations under the following headings: Literacy Instruction in First Through Third Grades, Promoting Literacy Development in Preschool and Kindergarten, Education and Professional Development for All Involved in Literacy Instruction, Teaching Reading to Speakers of Other Languages, Ensuring Adequate Resources to Meet Children's Needs, and Addressing the Needs of Children with Persistent Reading Difficulties.

Helping Children Overcome Reading Difficulties

http://www.indiana.edu/~reading/ieo/digests/d72.html

This Digest #72 from the *Clearinghouse on Reading, English, and Communication* provides teachers who are looking for a factual, research-based summary of current knowledge on reading difficulties with some excellent suggestions on how to help their students to overcome the problems of dyslexia.

READING RECOVERY

Reading Recovery

http://www.indiana.edu/~reading/ieo/digests/d106.html

In this *Clearinghouse on Reading, English, and Communication* Digest #106, Reading Recovery is described as a system of intense one-on-one assistance for students with reading difficulties, adapted from practices pioneered in New Zealand. It has been gaining popularity in the United States. The Digest's author, Roger Sensenbaugh, describes the program and some of the research dealing with it, and offers suggestions for further reading.

Reading Recovery Council of North America, 2004

http://www.readingrecovery.org/

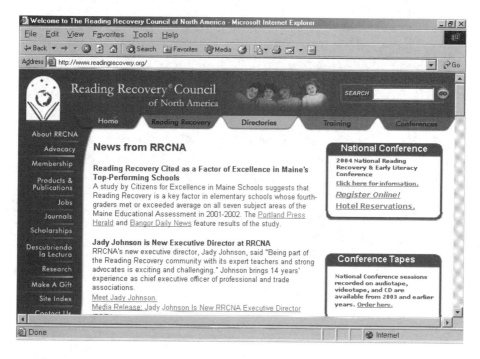

Reading Recovery Council of North America, 2004.

The website provided by the Reading Recovery Council of North America describes Reading Recovery as an early intervention designed to help children who are at the lowest levels of achievement in reading and writing to become proficient readers and writers. Reading Recovery assists first-grade children in catching up with their peers. The articles in this website are intended to provide basic information about reading recovery, to report on a variety of research and evaluation studies, and to provide access to articles that may be of interest to visitors to the site.

ADOLESCENT RELUCTANT READERS

http://www.allamericareads.org/

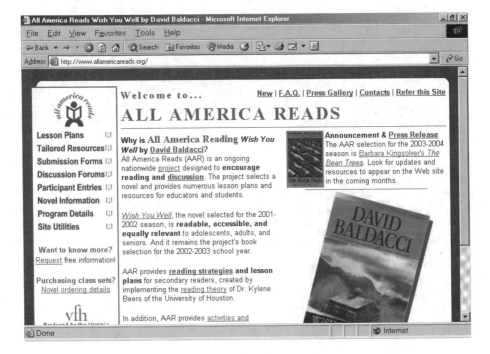

(Courtesy of the Virginia Foundation for the Humanities)

The *All America Reads* site is a wonderful resource for teachers of students in grades 6 to 12 who are reluctant to read. The site provides before, during, and after reading strategies as well as vocabulary and writing activities for students to work on as they read award-winning writer David Baldacci's young adult novel, *Wish You Well*. Baldacci's novel, which takes place in 1940, is a very powerful and yet easy-to-read tale about a 13-year-old girl named Lou Cardinal and her 8-year-old brother, Oz, who are forced to leave their home in New York to live with their grandmother in the mountains of rural Virginia after their father is killed in a car accident and their mother falls into a catatonic state. This exciting problem novel raises many social issues and deals with family and racial conflict. The reading theories of Dr. Kylene Beers of the University of Houston provide an excellent foundation for the strategies and activities which are provided to help students learn to read Baldacci's novel effectively. Even if you do not plan to use *Wish You Well* with your students, you should visit this site to see how to approach the teaching of young adult literature with reluctant readers.

GIFTED READERS

Gifted Readers and Reading Instruction

http://www.indiana.edu/~reading/ieo/digests/d101.html

In reviewing for the *Clearinghouse on Reading, English, & Communications* site, the professional literature on reading instruction for gifted readers, Norma Decker Collins and Nola Kortner Aiex have identified several salient points about gifted readers:

1. Gifted readers usually master basic reading skills by the time they come to school and are ready for complex concepts at an early age.
2. Gifted readers tend to have an internal locus of control—they believe that achievement is the result of their own ability and behavior.
3. Gifted readers need instruction in reading that is different from a regular classroom program.
4. Instruction for very able readers should focus on developing higher-cognitive-level comprehension skills.
5. Teaching reading to gifted readers requires more than a skills-oriented approach.
6. Books for gifted readers should be selected on the basis of quality language—books that use varied and complex language structures are a primary source of cognitive growth.
7. Reading programs for gifted readers should foster a desire to read.
8. A reading program for gifted readers should include a variety of reading materials and strategies that are based on the present needs and demands of the reader, not on the chronological age or grade level.

FUN WITH WORDS

Word Play

At these incredible sites your students can have fun with words. Here are five of the delightful activities that await K–12 students:

1. *American Slanguages:* Choose a city and learn to talk like the locals.
   http://www.slanguage.com/
2. *Brain Food:* Give your mind a workout with this devious collection of puzzles. There are hundreds, ranging from word games to logic problems to riddles. Some are tricky. Some require innovation. All require thinking power.
   http://rinkworks.com/brainfood/
3. *Create Your Own Shakespearean Insults:* Combine one word from each of three columns, preface with "Thou"—and thus shalt thou have the perfect insult. Let thyself go—mix and match to find a barb worthy of the Bard.
   http://www.dl.ket.org/humanities/connections/class/medren/insults.htm

4. *Stay Afloat:* Interactive game where you have to figure out the letters in a word before your boat sinks.
   http://www.funbrain.com/hangman/

5. *Little Explorers:* A multilingual (English; English–Spanish; English–French) picture dictionary with wonderful graphics and links.
   http://www.enchantedlearning.com/Dictionary.html

AltaVista Translation Service

http://babel.altavista.com/tr?

In this amazing translation site you write or cut and paste text into the space provided, and within seconds it is translated from English into French, Spanish, Portuguese, German, Italian, Chinese, or Japanese and vice versa. For real fun, try translating something into a second language and then back again into the original language.

STORYTIME

Childrenstory.com

http://www.childrenstory.com/tales/index.html

Here is a collection of many of the most popular fairy tales such as *Sleeping Beauty* and *Snow White.*

Heroes

http://www.mythweb.com/heroes/heroes.html

In this collection of ancient tales about Jason, Hercules, Odysseus, and others, the stories are illustrated with comical cartoon drawings that are certain to delight your students.

Mayan Folktales

http://www.folkart.com/~latitude/folktale/folktale.htm

Fernando Penalosa is a retired sociolinguist who most recently taught sociology, linguistics, and Chicano studies at California State University, Long Beach. For more than 12 years he has been working with Maya in Guatemala and the Los Angeles area, studying their languages and oral literature. On this site he presents his translations of the following Mayan tales: *The Disobedient Son, A Mayan Life, The Rabbit and the Coyote, The Rabbit Throws Out His Sandal,* and *The Jaguar and the Little Skunk.*

Native American Lore Index Page

http://www.ilhawaii.net/~stony/loreindx.html

This site contains more than 150 different Native American tales by Blackfoot, Mic-Mac, Cherokee, Hopi, Cheyenne, Iroquois, and many other First Nations storytellers.

Reading Rainbow

http://gpn.unl.edu/rainbow/

At this site students and teachers can learn more about the books that are featured on the popular *Reading Rainbow* television show. For instance, information on Episode 21 concerning the book *Paul Bunyan* by author/illustrator Steven Kellogg includes several Internet links to sites where students and teachers can learn more about Arbor Day. Also, there are lists of supplemental books such as *The Bunyans* for children who want to read more about this legendary hero of New England.

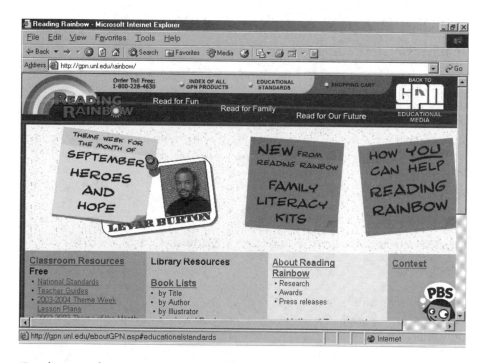

(Reading Rainbow is a production of the GPN/Nebraska ETV Network and WNED TV Buffalo)

Bedtime Stories

http://the-office.com/bedtime-story/

This award-winning site contains wonderfully illustrated web versions of many fine children's stories. The illustrations for *Alice In Wonderland,* for example, are both stunningly beautiful and humorous.

Recommended Youth Reading

http://www.st-charles.lib.il.us/low/ythread.htm

The St. Charles (IL) Public Library's Youth Services Division has compiled this set of more than 40 bibliographies on diverse topics such as sports, science fiction, and ghost stories, as well as books to help children cope with divorce, moving, the new baby, and child safety. There are also "read-alikes" for popular titles such as *Titanic Crossing.* Some of the lists are annotated.

LESSON PLANS FOR TEACHING READING

Teachers.Net Reading

http://www.teachers.net/cgi-bin/lessons/sort.cgi?searchterm=Reading

The *Teachers.Net Reading* site contains more than 150 lessons posted by participating teachers. For example, Dr. Candy Carlile's elementary reading lesson titled *Sight Word Soup* involves students in memorizing 10 new commonly used words each week by playing various games such as Bingo and Go Fish with them. The students then learn how to read the words in a sentence.

READING ACROSS THE CURRICULUM

http://teacher.scholastic.com/ilp/index.asp?SubjectID=1

Scholastic's *Reading and Language Arts* site contains many powerfully written online lessons and articles by leading writers in the field of reading research. For instance, Lucy Calkins, well-known director of the Teachers College Reading Project, has contributed an article titled "Let the Words Work Their Magic" about the power of reading aloud.

Improving Student Understanding of Textbook Content

http://www.ldonline.org/ld_indepth/teaching_techniques/understanding
_textbooks.html

This online article's textbook teaching and learning model is based on cognitive learning theory. It offers educators a new set of practices to show students how they may best learn the new content in three phases: before reading, during reading, and after reading. The article's author, Barbara Flanagan, offers a brief synopsis of the three phases and some teaching suggestions for each phase.

SUGGESTED ACTIVITIES

1. After reading some of the research articles in the first section of this chapter about learning to read, make a list of the additional strategies and beginning reading lessons you want to add to your own set of reading pedagogies. Then discuss your newly discovered theories and lesson plans with other reading teachers in your school. Of the seven promising reading programs examined by the American Federation of Teachers, which program do you think would best suit the needs of your students?

2. In the section of this chapter devoted to the never-ending battle between proponents of whole language and phonics there are several compelling arguments. Where do you situate yourself in this debate? What have you learned from these articles that will help you to defend your position when asking your principal for more teaching materials in the future?

3. From the research on reading disabilities mentioned in this chapter, develop a set of strategies that you intend to try with your dyslexic and ADHD students the next time you teach them reading.

4. Examine the sites and articles on reading recovery and gifted readers, and compare the approaches taken to these two groups of students in our schools. Then plan how you can accommodate both sets of students in your classroom at the same time.

5. Take a day with your students to play with some of the many fun-with-words sites mentioned in this chapter. For instance, you could have your students use the Altavista translator to write e-mail messages to students in France, Germany, and Mexico. Or you could use it to help them translate poems from French or Spanish into English.

6. Take your elementary students to visit one of the many story sites mentioned in this chapter, and encourage them to each select a different story to retell to the class. Where possible, enable the students to use the illustrations to help them remember how their selected story goes.

7. Choose a dozen lesson plans from the reading lesson plan sites discussed in this chapter, and use them as the foundation for preparing a theme unit to teach to your class.

8. After studying, with the help of the *All America Reads* site, some of the lesson plans that were written for the novel, *Wish You Well,* use these lessons as models for a unit you are teaching to your reluctant adolescent readers. Prepare some pre-reading, during-reading, and post-reading activities to guide your students through their study of their novel.

SUMMARY

Given the volume of research in the area of reading, it is difficult to remain informed about the latest changes in the field. That is why it is reassuring to find articles and monographs by respected writers in reading research such as Lucy Calkins, Kylene Beers, and the many other fine reading specialists whose works we have reviewed in this chapter. Similarly, given the isolated nature of our work as reading teachers, it is good to know that we can enter discussion groups on the Internet through organizations such as the NCTE's Whole Language Umbrella to share our concerns and suggestions with colleagues around the globe. Finally, once we have gained some confidence in our theories about teaching learning-disabled and gifted readers, it is truly exciting to realize that sites such as *Childrenstory.com* are available to provide us with literature that is a pleasure to teach to these young scholars.

CHAPTER 4

Literature for Children and Adolescents

- Children's Literature
- Young Adult Literature
- Mythology
- Poetry
- Short Stories
- Novels
- Drama
- British Authors
- American Authors
- Canadian Authors
- Multicultural and World Literature Authors

CHILDREN'S LITERATURE

When you were a child reading or viewing *The Wizard of Oz*, did you ever wonder about tornado warning signs or about what to do if you were caught in a tornado? In this chapter you will not only have those questions answered for you, but you will also be able to consider geographical, artistic, and historical topics associated with Frank Baum's writings. Opportunities on the Internet abound for intertextually linking ideas, sounds, and images to the literature we love to read and teach. Thus, in this chapter, which contains a large collection of literature sites that are in turn linked to thousands of other sites, we hope to make the point that interdisciplinary learning is now easier than ever to achieve with your students through the magic of hypertextuality.

Another way in which the intertextual nature of the Internet may enhance your teaching can be found in the amazing links that are made across and within cultures, whether these connections are made among various children's stories around the world or among the different versions of a single story such as *Snow White*.

Several fine, comprehensive sites are discussed in this chapter, such as *The Children's Literature Web Guide* and the *Dramatic Exchange*. Through these sites you can find your way to thousands of works of literature. We present here as well sites containing students' creative writing and responses to literature. And you will find in this chapter sites devoted to many of your favorite authors of children's and young adult literature, as well as web pages devoted to the classic writers taught in secondary schools, such as John Steinbeck and William Shakespeare.

Through the mythology sites listed here, your students can explore the similarities among heroes in Greek, Norse, Chinese, and Iroquois tales. Or they can create their own legendary monsters after reading about the werewolves and goblins described in these sites.

After studying haiku written by Japanese poets and by children around the world, your students can write their own poems and post them on the Internet. If you are at a loss for ideas about teaching poetry or for examples of good poetry, sites such as the *Glossary of Poetic Terms* and *Twentieth-century Poetry in English* will help you find what you need.

As you read this chapter, therefore, we suggest that you consider how best to make use of the resources here to involve your students in making their own connections across disciplines and cultures. In the first section, for instance, as you study the various children's literature sites we have selected, ask yourself how your students might be able to better appreciate the work of authors such as Hans Christian Andersen, Beverly Cleary, and Roald Dahl by following some of the links in the sites devoted to their work. In the case of Dahl's site, for example, how might your students come to appreciate his stories better by taking part in the activities recommended by the teachers who have contributed their ideas to the site?

The Children's Literature Web Guide

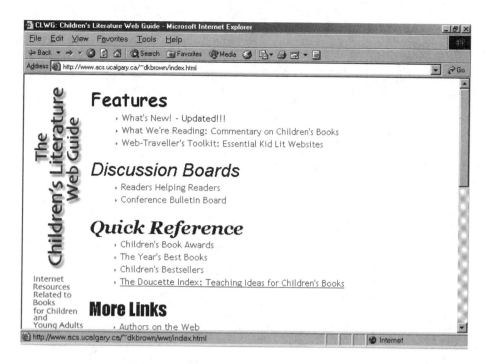

http://www.acs.ucalgary.ca/~dkbrown/index.html	
Intended Audience	Teachers and students
Grade Level	K–12
Curricular Fit	Children's and young adult literature
Types of Resources	Biographical information on authors, lesson plans, book lists
Authorship of Site	David K. Brown at the University of Calgary
Navigation	Good
Visual Appeal	Good
Interactive Activity	Some opportunity for teachers and students to review books

The *Children's Literature Web Guide* is an excellent place to start your search for children's and young adult literature resources and links. This comprehensive site contains teaching resources such as lesson plans for some books, biographical information about authors, lists of award-winning and best-selling books, a conference bulletin board, journals, book reviews, discussion groups, research guides, children's literature organizations, children's publishers, and book sellers. This site also provides links to many other valuable children's literature sites such as Carol Hurst's *Children's Literature Web Site,* Kay Vandergrift's *Special Interest Page,* and *OzKidz*

Literature. If you would like to learn how to write or illustrate children's literature yourself, try the link to *The Purple Crayon,* where you can read advice from children's book editor Harold Underdown.

The next two sites also provide good general lists of information from which you can look for specific details about authors. After describing these two sites we provide a sampling of 15 other web pages about particular writers or genres of children's literature. Most of these sites are of more use to you than to your students. They enable you to learn about the lives and works of famous children's book writers such as Beverly Cleary and L. M. Montgomery. But some, as we shall point out, are written with your students in mind and are very interactive.

Great Web Sites for Kids: Favorite Children's Stories

http://www.ala.org/Content/NavigationMenu/ALSC/Great_Web_Sites _for_Kids/Great_Web_Sites__Favorite_Childrens_Stories.htm	
Intended Audience	Teachers
Grade Level	K–8
Curricular Fit	Children's literature
Types of Resources	Lists of links about favorite children's stories, authors
Authorship of Site	American Library Association
Navigation	Good
Visual Appeal	Fair
Interactive Activity	None

At the *Great Web Sites for Kids: Favorite Children's Stories,* the Association for Library Service to Children has brought together a fascinating list of sites under the categories of Favorite Children's Stories. Here you can find links to sites devoted to children's book series such as *The Baby-Sitters' Club* and the *Berenstain Bears.* For the Narnia books, you can find a very detailed and extensive description of the creatures and history of C. S. Lewis' imaginary land by traveling through the *Explore Narnia* porthole.

Learning About the Author and Illustrator Pages

http://www.scils.rutgers.edu/~kvander/AuthorSite/	
Intended Audience	Teachers and students
Grade Level	4–12
Curricular Fit	Children's and young adult literature
Types of Resources	Biographical and literary sites
Authorship of Site	Kay Vandergrift
Navigation	Good
Visual Appeal	Good
Interactive Activity	None

Included in the more than 600 sites listed in Kay Vandergrift's *Learning About the Author and Illustrator Pages* are authors and illustrators of children's and young adult books as well as many authors of adult books that are commonly read by older children. As Kay explains, the author/illustrator sites included are not intended to contain comprehensive information about particular authors/illustrators. Rather, some contain biographical, bibliographic, and critical data along with personal responses to selected works, while others provide a small taste of an author's/illustrator's work. This is a rich source of information about the authors (and illustrators) of children's and young adult books from Lloyd Alexander to Paul Zindel.

Wonderful Wizard of Oz

http://www.eskimo.com/~tiktok/index.html	
Intended Audience	Teachers
Grade Level	4–8
Curricular Fit	Children's fantasy literature
Types of Resources	Excellent set of lessons for theme unit
Authorship of Site	Eric Gjovaag
Navigation	Good
Visual Appeal	Good
Interactive Activity	None

Eric Gjovaag's *Wonderful Wizard of Oz* website contains many fine illustrations and images from various editions of Frank Baum's book and the famous movie that was made from it. At this site you can also discuss Baum's books by joining an e-mail list. Furthermore, you can download an excellent set of theme unit activities that combine activities for science, health, geography, history, mathematics, language arts, art, music, technology, social and life skills, home economics, and psychology. In the list of science activities, for instance, Gjovaag suggests that students get carried away with a study of tornadoes. They can visit a linked tornado page telling them the tornado warning signs and what to do if they are ever caught in a tornado.

Among the language arts activities recommended by Gjovaag is to encourage students to write their own, original Oz adventures. The students can even make themselves the main characters! How did they get there? Who did they meet? What problems did they encounter? How do they get home? The possible story lines are endless.

Snow White

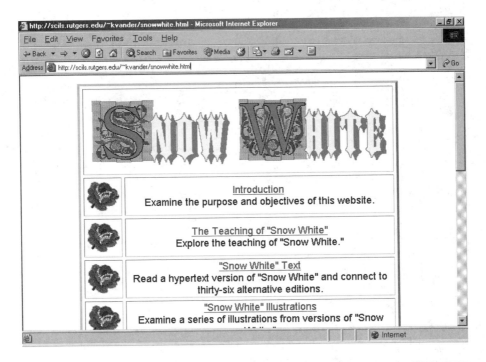

http://scils.rutgers.edu/~kvander/snowwhite.html	
Intended Audience	Teachers
Grade Level	University Children's Literature course
Curricular Fit	Fairy tales and folklore
Types of Resources	Critical analyses of Snow White
Authorship of Site	Kay Vandergrift
Navigation	Good
Visual Appeal	Fair
Interactive Activity	None

While the site *Snow White* does not give much direct assistance to those who wish to teach the story to their students, it does provide important critical perspectives on the various versions of the story as well as thought-provoking questions for teachers to consider, such as the following:

- What are the differences among the textual interpretations of the story?
- Are the different versions intended for different audiences?
- How do these versions compare with the earliest available written form of the story?
- What are the differences among the visual interpretations of the story?
- Is the specific content of the story altered in any way by the illustrations? If so, how (character, mood, plot, etc.)?
- What is the relationship, if any, between illustrative technique and mood in the story? Between color and mood?
- How are the visual details of setting used in the storytelling?
- Is the number of illustrations and their placement in relation to the text appropriate to the story?
- Do visual and verbal points of view correspond and complement each other?
- Is the format of the book as a physical object part of its affective statement as story?

Storytime

http://pbskids.org/retired_storytime.html	
Intended Audience	Teachers and parents
Grade Level	K–2
Curricular Fit	Early literacy
Types of Resources	Short descriptions of story books, literacy advice for parents
Authorship of Site	KCET and PBS
Navigation	Good
Visual Appeal	Good
Interactive Activity	None

The *Storytime* site provides short descriptions of the books that have been read on the PBS television show *Storytime*. Here parents and teachers of primary students can also read helpful suggestions about how to raise their children's literacy levels.

Aesop's Fables Online Collection

http://www.pacificnet.net/~johnr/aesop/	
Intended Audience	Teachers and students
Grade Level	2–10
Curricular Fit	Folklore, fairy tales, and fables
Types of Resources	Audio clips, electronic texts, illustrations of the tales
Authorship of Site	John R. Long of Star Systems
Navigation	Good
Visual Appeal	Good
Interactive Activity	Listening to stories and viewing illustrations

Included among the more than 650 fables at *Aesop's Fables Online Collection* are Real Audio narrations, classic images, random images, random fables, a search engine, a message forum, and much more on the way. This site also offers 127 fairy tales by Hans Christian Andersen. A particularly endearing feature of the site, which will undoubtedly appeal to younger children, is the narration provided on Real Audio by Heather Long, the 10-year-old daughter of the website's author, John Long.

Reading Zone

http://www.ipl.org/div/kidspace/browse/rzn0000/	
Intended Audience	Students
Grade Level	4–9
Curricular Fit	Reading
Types of Resources	Picture books, short stories, and poetry
Authorship of Site	Internet Public Library Youth Division
Navigation	Good
Visual Appeal	Good
Interactive Activity	Some opportunity to take part in discussion groups

When your students visit the Internet Public Library's *Reading Zone* site they can learn how braille works or read animated picture books. They can also submit their poems and stories to a creative writing site where they can also read the work of other young writers like themselves. At the *Reading Zone*'s Resources for Teachers and Parents area, materials are available to help children to learn to read.

Story Place

http://www.storyplace.org/	
Intended Audience	Teachers and students
Grade Level	Preschool to grade 3
Curricular Fit	Reading activities
Types of Resources	Animated stories, activities
Authorship of Site	Public Library of Charlotte and Mecklenburg County
Navigation	Good
Visual Appeal	Good
Interactive Activity	Listening to the stories and viewing the animation

Story Place is an educational activity center for children. The stories at this site have sound and animation. There are enjoyable activities for children, all with an educational focus. The site also provides themed lists of additional books for children to read.

The World of Beverly Cleary

http://www.beverlycleary.com/	
Intended Audience	Teachers and students
Grade Level	4–8
Curricular Fit	Children's literature
Types of Resources	Biography, book descriptions, FAQs
Authorship of Site	HarperCollins Publishing Co.
Navigation	Good
Visual Appeal	Good
Interactive Activity	None

If your students want to learn more about Cleary's wonderful characters, such as Beezus and Ramona Quimby or Henry Huggins, this site has a page (still under construction at the time of this writing) that answers such questions as, "How much is Ramona like her creator?"

L. M. Montgomery Institute

Copyright L. M. Montgomery Institute of UPEI, 2002.

http://www.upei.ca/~lmmi/	
Intended Audience	Teachers
Grade Level	5 9
Curricular Fit	Canadian literature
Types of Resources	Conferences and teacher resources on books and films
Authorship of Site	L. M. Montgomery Institute
Navigation	Good
Visual Appeal	Good
Interactive Activity	None

The *L. M. Montgomery Institute,* dedicated to Lucy Maud Montgomery, provides you with information about her internationally acclaimed books such as *Anne of Green Gables* and *Emily of New Moon.*

Baby-sitters Club Author, Ann M. Martin's, Homepage at *Scholastic*

http://www.scholastic.com/annmartin/index.htm	
Intended Audience	Ann M. Martin's fan's
Grade Level	Grades 3–8
Curricular Fit	Children's literature
Types of Resources	Info on books and biographical info about Ann M. Martin
Authorship of Site	Ann M. Martin
Navigation	Good
Visual Appeal	Good
Interactive Activity	Good

At *Scholastics' Kids Fun Online* site you can find web pages devoted to the prolific author of the *Baby-sitters Club* and *The Baby-sitters Little Sister Series,* Ann M. Martin. By reading Ann's letters to her fans you can learn, for instance, that she recently won a Newbury Honor for her book, *A Corner of the Universe,* which is about a 12-year-old girl named Hattie who develops a relationship with her schizophrenic and autistic Uncle Adam. Ann regularly responds to e-mails from her young readers and her replies to selected questions are posted on this site. The site also contains character sketches of the members of the Baby-sitters Club as well as descriptions of many of her books.

The Official Roald Dahl Web Site

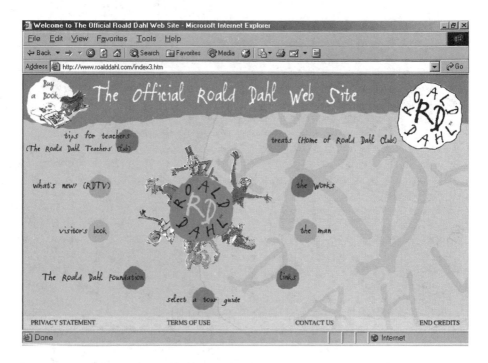

http://www.roalddahl.com/index3.htm	
Intended Audience	Teachers and students
Grade Level	K–9
Curricular Fit	Children's and young adult literature
Types of Resources	Bio, articles, movie clips, games
Authorship of Site	Dahl and Dahl, the Roald Dahl Literary Estate
Navigation	Good
Visual Appeal	Good
Interactive Activity	Voice of Sophie Dahl engages visitors in dialogue, Roald Dahl challenge game

The Official Roald Dahl Web Site contains many imaginative features to help you come to know Roald Dahl and his books. For instance, you can listen to an interview made with Dahl when he was 71 years old in which he answers questions such as "Where did you get the idea for *James and the Giant Peach?*" The voice of Sophie Dahl is used throughout the site to guide visitors. Besides the biographical information and articles about Dahl's writing, you can find a number of reviews of his books (*Matilda* and *Willy Wonka and the Chocolate Factory*) by visitors to the site. There are video clips of movies that were based upon his books and a delightful game called The Roald Dahl Challenge to entertain young fans of Dahl's books.

Patricia Polacco.com

http://www.patriciapolacco.com/	
Intended Audience	Teachers and students
Grade Level	K–6
Curricular Fit	Multicultural picture books
Types of Resources	Teaching ideas, book synopsis, artwork samples
Authorship of Site	Steven Polacco
Navigation	Good
Visual Appeal	Good
Interactive Activity	Quizzes, puzzles, color-ins, electronic postcards, video gallery, chats, contests.

Patricia Polacco, author of 36 beautiful, heart-warming picture books, and her website developer, Steven Polacco, have constructed an amazing homepage, which contains helpful teaching ideas for educators and many enjoyable activities such as puzzles and quizzes for young students. A synopsis and samples of artwork are provided for all Patricia's books. You will also find detailed lesson plans for several of her stories. For instance, for *Mr. Lincoln's Way*, a story about a young bully who learns to overcome his racist tendencies when his African American principal invites him to help to attract birds to the school atrium, the lesson devoted to this story asks: "What was Mr. Lincoln hoping to accomplish by inviting Eugene to help attract birds to the school atrium? Does the idea that many different types of birds can live and survive peacefully together, act as a metaphor for our nation? How so?" Teachers and students can also gather together online to discuss Polacco's books in the chat room, or they can read quotations from students on selected topics such as Acts of Kindness, Prized Possessions, Dreams, and Growing Up.

Sharon Creech

http://www.sharoncreech.com/index.html	
Intended Audience	Teachers and students
Grade Level	K–8
Curricular Fit	Children's and young adult literature
Types of Resources	Literature Circle teaching ideas, autobiographical connections to books, audio files of book excerpts, sample chapters
Authorship of Site	Sharon Creech
Navigation	Good
Visual Appeal	Good
Interactive Activity	None

Sharon Creech won the Newbery Award in 1995 for her novel, *Walk Two Moons,* about a 13-year-old girl from Kentucky named Salamanca Tree Hiddle, who tells fascinating stories to her grandparents while she travels with them to Idaho. Equally successful at writing for children and young adults, Sharon's novels and picture books are often related to events in her personal life that she recounts in this web site. As well as audio clips and sample chapters from her stories, she has included a PDF file of literature circle teaching ideas titled *Teach Creech.* In this document, which uses Creech's novel, *Pleasing the Ghost* for examples, you will read the role definitions for the following literature circle group members: director, passage detective, researcher, connector, and vocabulary enricher.

Robert Munsch

http://www.robertmunsch.com/	
Intended Audience	Teachers and students
Grade Level	K–4
Curricular Fit	Picture books
Types of Resources	Background discussions of his stories as well as audio files of Robert telling his stories
Authorship of Site	Robert Munsch
Navigation	Good
Visual Appeal	Good
Interactive Activity	Listening to Robert's stories, viewing artwork and photographs

Robert Munsch's books, such as *The Paper Bag Princess* and *Love You Forever,* have sold millions of copies. One reason why Robert's story-telling is so powerful is that, for the past thirty years, he has refined his stories by telling them to young children in day care centers and elementary schools across North America. Now your students can hear Robert's wildly funny and touchingly sad tales in his own voice by visiting the Virtual Story Room area at his homepage. You can also view pictures of Robert telling his stories to some of the classes that he has visited. This site has many other exciting features to discover including the artwork that students have submitted. In the Something Special area, many treats abound such as the photographic story that Robert tells of his surprise visit to a school on Bowen Island near Vancouver.

Newbery Medal Homepage

http://www.ala.org/Content/NavigationMenu/ALSC/Awards_and _Scholarships1/Literary_and_Related_Awards/Newbery_Medal/Newbery _Medal.htm	
Intended Audience	Teachers and students
Grade Level	K–8
Curricular Fit	Literature study
Types of Resources	List of Newbury Award Winners since 1922, Caldecott and other awards as well
Authorship of Site	Association for Library Service to Children
Navigation	Good
Visual Appeal	Fair
Interactive Activity	None

The *Newbery Medal Homepage* is just one of many related pages provided by the Association for Library Service to Children. Besides being able to read a list of all of the Newbery Medal winners from 1922 to the present, you can also gain access to information about the Caldecott and Wilder Awards for children's literature, and about the Carnegie Award for children's video. The 2003 winner of the Newbery Award was Avi, whose action-packed YA novel, *Crispin: The Cross of Lead,* takes place in fourteenth-century England. Crispin is a 13-year-old orphan boy fleeing for his life across England because his enemies have wrongly accused him of murder. Some other famous Newbery award–winning authors listed at this site include Sharon Creech, Lois Lowry, and Beverly Cleary.

Edward Lear Homepage

http://www.nonsenselit.org/Lear/	
Intended Audience	Teachers and students
Grade Level	K–12
Curricular Fit	Nonsense poetry
Types of Resources	Lear's complete limericks and links to related sites
Authorship of Site	Marco Graziosi
Navigation	Good
Visual Appeal	Good
Interactive Activity	None

Marco Graziosi, the author of the *Edward Lear Homepage,* has written a thesis about Lear's nonsense verse, and he wanted to make the poems and Lear's biography available to fellow Lear devotees on the Internet. As Graziosi puts it, "If you share the

Jumblies' spirit of adventure or your nose is as luminous as the Dong's, if you think there's nothing strange in living in the nest of an owl or your feelings are wrung with compunction, go on" and enjoy this wonderfully humorous site.

YOUNG ADULT LITERATURE

Authors 4 Teens.com

http://www.authors4teens.com/default.htm	
Intended Audience	Teachers and students
Grade Level	Teachers and students grades 7–12
Curricular Fit	Young adult literature
Types of Resources	Short descriptions of books, author biographies, interviews, links to YA book sites, webboard
Authorship of Site	Teri Lesesne
Navigation	Good
Visual Appeal	Good
Interactive Activity	None

At the *Authors 4 Teens* site, through online biographies, interviews, and links to author web sites, you can introduce your students to more than 40 popular YA authors such as Chris Crutcher, Jane Yolen, and Paul Zindel. In Teri's Corner, Teri Lesesne, who teaches courses in Young Adult Literature at Sam Houston State University, provides a newsletter in which she includes book talks, conference announcements, list of current popular books, story collections worth collecting. This site also contains a frequently asked questions area and a webboard where students and teachers can discuss their favorite authors.

The ISLMC's Children's and Young Adults' Authors & Illustrators

http://falcon.jmu.edu/~ramseyil/biochildhome.htm	
Intended Audience	Teachers and students
Grade Level	K–12
Curricular Fit	Children's and young adult literature
Types of Resources	Bibliographies, biographies, and book reviews
Authorship of Site	Inez Ramsey for the Internet School Library Media Center
Navigation	Good
Visual Appeal	Good
Interactive Activity	None

Inez Ramsey's extensive list of authors of children's and young adult books on the ISLMC Index not only provides excellent biographical and bibliographical materials for each author but also supplies teacher resources for many of the writers as well. In the case of Lois Lowry, for example, you will find eight different brief biographies, a list of 24 books by Lowry, and 10 teachers' guides about her work. You can also read online reviews of her books and choose from more than 10 unit plans. One of these, on *The Giver*, includes the opportunity for students to listen to an audio file of Lowry discussing her reasons for ending the story as she did before being encouraged to write their own ending to the novel. Inez Ramsey's site is indeed a thorough and valuable resource for K–12 teachers of literature.

Canadian Young Adult Literature

http://www.publib.saskatoon.sk.ca/reference.html	
Intended Audience	Teachers and students
Grade Level	8–12
Curricular Fit	Canadian young adult literature
Types of Resources	Author biographies, book reviews
Authorship of Site	Maureen Arnason
Navigation	Fair
Visual Appeal	Fair
Interactive Activity	None

The *Canadian Young Adult Literature* site is very helpful in providing basic biographies of Canadian writers of young adult literature and reviews of their books;

however, it does not provide links to related sites or teacher resources and lesson plans. Nevertheless, if you use this site as a starting point to identify who the authors are, you can then do a *Yahoo* search in order to discover that several of these writers have their own websites, such as the following homepage of Kevin Major.

The Novels of Kevin Major

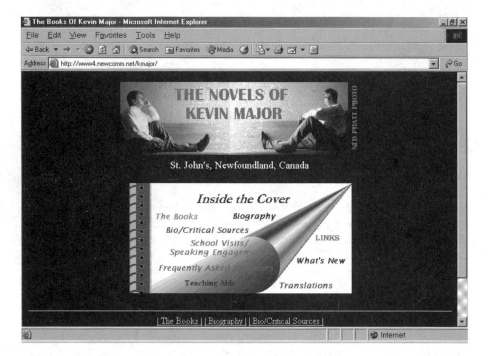

http://www4.newcomm.net/kmajor/	
Intended Audience	Teachers and students
Grade Level	6–10
Curricular Fit	Young adult literature
Types of Resources	Biographical and bibliographical info and teaching guides
Authorship of Site	Kevin Major
Navigation	Good
Visual Appeal	Good
Interactive Activity	Students can write the author or visit related sites

Kevin Major is a Newfoundland writer of such popular young adult novels as *Diana: My Autobiography.* For four of his novels he provides teaching guides that contain imaginative English language arts and social studies activities as well as interesting links to other sites on the Internet. For example, for *Blood Red Ochre*, his time-travel novel about the extinction of the Beothuk Aboriginal people of Newfoundland, he suggests that students consider what might have happened had the Beothuks survived. He also provides a link to the Newfoundland and Labrador website, where they can read about the Beothuk people and view some of their artifacts.

S. E. Hinton

http://www.sehinton.com/	
Intended Audience	Teachers and students
Grade Level	7–12
Curricular Fit	Young adult high-action literature
Types of Resources	Excerpts from books, Hinton's biography, FAQs, movies, Hinton's personal reflections
Authorship of Site	Teknospace Design and S. E. Hinton
Navigation	Good
Visual Appeal	Fair
Interactive Activity	Students can write the author

Susan Hinton's official web site contains wonderful reflections by the author about her books and the movies that are based upon them. The site provides a biography of the author as well as her answers to frequently asked questions that have been written in by young readers. This site is essential for fans of Hinton's ground-breaking books such as *The Outsiders*.

Random House's Teachers@Random

http://www.randomhouse.com/teachers/index.html	
Intended Audience	Teachers
Grade Level	K–12
Curricular Fit	Young adult literature
Types of Resources	Teaching guides for hundreds of Random House novels
Authorship of Site	Random House
Navigation	Good
Visual Appeal	Fair
Interactive Activity	None

Random House's Index provides a list of teaching resources for hundreds of young adult novels by such well-known authors as Madeleine L'Engle, S. E. Hinton, and Gary Paulsen. It enables, for instance, teachers of the Hinton novels, *Tex, Rumble*

Fish, and *Taming the Star Runner,* to encourage their students to consider the themes of acceptance, family relationships, self-esteem, and self-discovery in these three books, as well as to examine interdisciplinary links with history and science.

Welcome to Jack London's Ranch Album

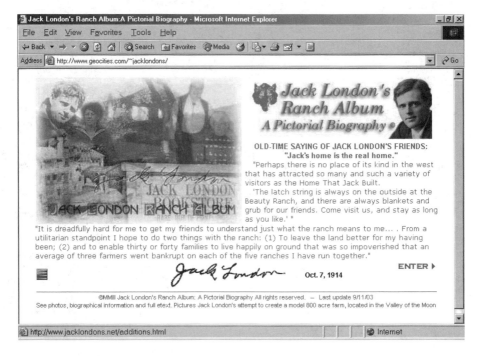

Jack London's Ranch Album: A Pictorial Biography

http://www.jacklondons.net	
Intended Audience	Teachers
Grade Level	6–12
Curricular Fit	Young adult fiction
Types of Resources	Pictures, biography, electronic versions of London's books
Authorship of Site	David Hartzell
Navigation	Good
Visual Appeal	Good
Interactive Activity	None

This site is an excellent resource for students who want to read Jack London's books and to learn about his adventurous life. Among the texts students can read here in electronic form are *The Call of the Wild, The Sea-Wolf,* and *Selected Klondike Stories.*

They can also learn about the model farm that London was working on before he died at the age of 40.

Gary Paulsen

http://www.randomhouse.com/features/garypaulsen/	
Intended Audience	Teachers and students
Grade Level	6–10
Curricular Fit	Young adult literature
Types of Resources	Biography of Paulsen and descriptions of his books
Authorship of Site	Random House
Navigation	Good
Visual Appeal	Good
Interactive Activity	None

At Gary Paulsen's site students can read about Gary's exciting boat trips, and they can send him questions about his novel *Hatchet* and the sequel, *Brian's Return*. They can also visit the Library section of the site to learn about some of Paulsen's other novels.

Lois Lowry

http://www.loislowry.com/	
Intended Audience	Teachers and students
Grade Level	7–10
Curricular Fit	Young adult literature
Types of Resources	Author biography and book summaries
Authorship of Site	Lois Lowry
Navigation	Good
Visual Appeal	Good
Interactive Activity	None

On the first page of Lois Lowry's site she says that she wishes she could invite her readers into her kitchen for a visit, but that perhaps interacting at her site can serve the same purpose. By the time you have finished reading her speeches, perusing the synopses of her many wonderful books, such as *The Giver,* and learning in her biography about how her son, a fighter pilot, sadly died in a plane crash, you will feel that you have actually spent some time with Lois. But, in case you still have questions for her that have not been answered in her frequently asked questions page, you can write her an e-mail message.

Lord of the Flies

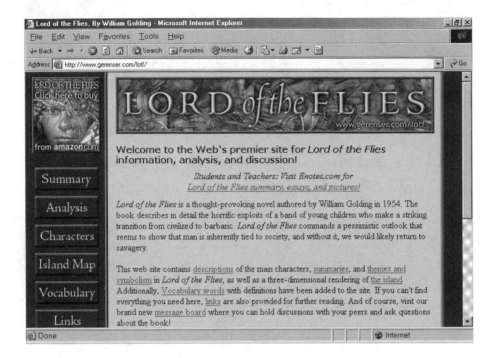

http://www.gerenser.com/lotf/	
Intended Audience	Teachers and students
Grade Level	10–12
Curricular Fit	Young adult literature
Types of Resources	Author bio, overview, character sketches, symbolism chart
Authorship of Site	Scott Gerenser
Navigation	Good
Visual Appeal	Good
Interactive Activity	Discussion forum

Students who visit the *Lord of the Flies* site can study vocabulary lists for each chapter, post their ideas and questions about the book on a discussion forum, read summaries of the book's chapters, see photographs and read descriptions of the main characters, and follow links to sites about the life of the book's author, William Golding.

One Ring: The Complete Guide to Tolkien Online

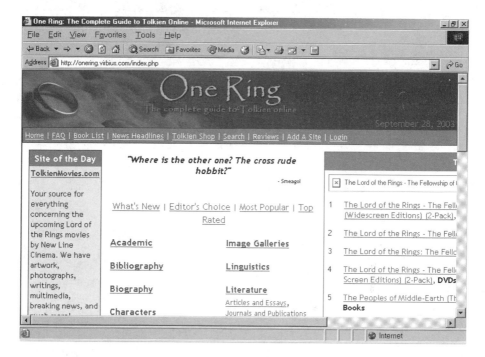

http://onering.virbius.com/index.php	
Intended Audience	Teachers and students
Grade Level	6–12
Curricular Fit	Young adult literature
Types of Resources	Links to dozens of Tolkien sites
Authorship of Site	Darryl Friesen
Navigation	Good
Visual Appeal	Good
Interactive Activity	Games and a recording of Tolkien's last interview

This complete guide to *The Lord of the Rings* provides links to dozens of other sites about Tolkien's books. There are many links to articles, elvish fonts, graphics, games, and music. This page also provides extensive lists of Tolkien newsgroups, periodicals, and societies, as well as links to linguistics sites about the languages in Tolkien's novels. Another interesting site that is also by Darryl Friesen is *The Tolkien Timeline* at **http://gollum.usask.ca/tolkien/**.

The SF Site: The Home Page for Science Fiction and Fantasy

http://www.sfsite.com/home.htm	
Intended Audience	Science fiction readers of all ages
Grade Level	8–12
Curricular Fit	Young adult literature
Types of Resources	Book reviews, ezines, art galleries, interviews with authors, links to author web pages
Authorship of Site	Rodger Turner
Navigation	Good
Visual Appeal	Good
Interactive Activity	None

The *SF Site* contains a wonderful list of links to sites that are of interest to those who love to read and view science fiction and fantasy. The author sites that are connected to the *SF Site* include such famous writers as Lloyd Alexander, Ray Bradbury, Ursula K. Le Guin, and Stephen King. Other features that make this one of the best science fiction and fantasy sites on the Internet are: book reviews, interviews, novel excerpts, science fact, ezines, magazines, conventions, topical lists, art galleries, computer games, TV shows, movies (*Star Wars, Star Trek,* etc.), comics, and audiotapes.

Ray Bradbury

http://www.raybradbury.com/	
Intended Audience	Science fiction readers of all ages
Grade Level	8–12
Curricular Fit	Young adult fiction
Types of Resources	A wealth of biographical and literary information about Bradbury and his works
Authorship of Site	HarperCollins Publishers
Navigation	Good
Visual Appeal	Good
Interactive Activity	Video clips and message board.

At the *Ray Bradbury* site students can view a series of video clips in which Ray, seated at the desk in his basement where he has written more than 500 literary works over the past 60 years, talks about his novels such as *Fahrenheit 451, The Martian Chronicles,* and *Dandelion Wine.* They can also read excerpts from many of his books as well as articles about Bradbury's work. One of the most charming essays by Bradbury himself involves his description of the day when he was twelve years old that he decided to become a writer after having a mystical chat with a magician at a circus.

Arthur C. Clarke Unauthorized Homepage

http://www.lsi.usp.br/~rbianchi/clarke/	
Intended Audience	Adolescent science fiction readers
Grade Level	8–12
Curricular Fit	Young adult literature
Types of Resources	Biography, bibliography, filmography, interviews
Authorship of Site	Reinaldo Bianchi
Navigation	Good
Visual Appeal	Good
Interactive Activity	None

This site contains a large collection of sites about the author and his works as well as links to information about the films that have been based upon his novels, such as *2001: A Space Odyssey*. Students with a real interest in Clarke's work may wish to join the Arthur C. Clarke Fan Club.

Robert Heinlein: Dean of Science Fiction Writers

http://www.wegrokit.com	
Intended Audience	Science fiction readers
Grade Level	7–12
Curricular Fit	Young adult literature
Types of Resources	Biography, bibliography, audio file, bulletin board, news
Authorship of Site	Lizbeth Ager and Carlos Angelo
Navigation	Good
Visual Appeal	Good
Interactive Activity	Listening to radio show

This site provides an examination of Heinlein's life and legacy and an extensive collection of book reviews, excerpts, and book covers. Essays about Heinlein, his works and his influence, a bulletin board, and the weekly *Heinlein News* all combine to furnish readers with a rich assortment of background materials with which to assess his fiction. Among the many related sites linked to this one are an audio file of a radio play version of Heinlein's classic short story, "The Roads Must Roll," and a New Age Church of All Worlds named after a church in Heinlein's novel, *Stranger in a Strange Land*.

Isaac Asimov Homepage

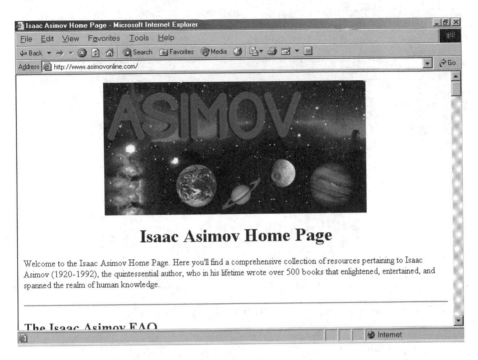

http://www.asimovonline.com/	
Intended Audience	Science fiction readers
Grade Level	8–12
Curricular Fit	Young adult literature
Types of Resources	FAQs, descriptions of his books, reviews, audio files
Authorship of Site	Edward Seiler
Navigation	Good
Visual Appeal	Good
Interactive Activity	None

Because Isaac Asimov wrote over 500 books during his lifetime, it is understandable that this site dedicated to his works would be so rich with information. From here your students can download a transcript and audio file of a speech delivered by Asimov, they can read reviews and essays about his more famous books such as the *Foundation* series, and they can read answers to a huge list of FAQs about his life and work. Among the related sites available through the homepage is the electronic magazine titled *Science Fiction Weekly*.

The Official Ursula K. Le Guin Homepage

http://www.ursulakleguin.com/	
Intended Audience	Teachers and students
Grade Level	4–12
Curricular Fit	Children's and Young Adult Science Fiction
Types of Resources	Biography, bibliography, interviews, performances, reviews
Authorship of Site	Ursula K. Le Guin
Navigation	Good
Visual Appeal	Fair
Interactive Activity	None

Ursula Le Guin has written 16 novels, 4 collections of poetry, 10 children's books, several screenplays, and more. This site provides brief descriptions of Le Guin's children's and young adult science fiction books as well as discussions about television performances of her book *The Lathe of Heaven*. It includes reviews of her work as well as etext samples of her short stories, poems, essays, and translations. In the frequently asked questions sections, Le Guin describes her childhood interest in writing. Ursula Le Guin's nomination for a Nebula award in 2001 for her latest Earthsea novel, *The Other Wind*, and her nomination for a Hugo award in 2003 for her novelette, *The Wild Girls*, both indicate that she is still one of the world's finest writers of science fiction.

MYTHOLOGY

The Encyclopedia Mythica

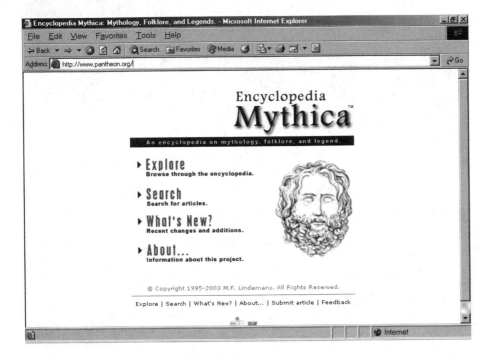

http://www.pantheon.org/	
Intended Audience	Teachers and students
Grade Level	4–12
Curricular Fit	Mythology
Types of Resources	Articles, images, maps, genealogical tables, links
Authorship of Site	M. F. Lindemans
Navigation	Good
Visual Appeal	Good
Interactive Activity	None

The *Encyclopedia Mythica* contains over 4,700 articles on mythological characters from around the world. Greek, Chinese, Aztec, Hindu, and Celtic mythologies are just a few of the many represented here. Students can also view over 200 beautiful illustrations, maps, and genealogical tables.

Odin's Castle of Dreams and Legends: An Archive of History and Historical Resources

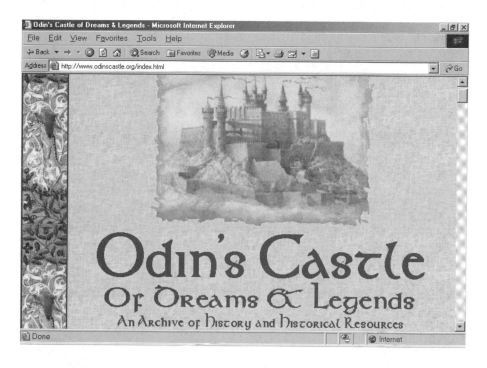

http://www.odinscastle.org/index.html	
Intended Audience	Teachers and students
Grade Level	6–12
Curricular Fit	Interdisciplinary theme units: mythology, legends, history
Types of Resources	Links to mythological and historical sites
Authorship of Site	Paul Gwynn
Navigation	Good
Visual Appeal	Good
Interactive Activity	None

Odin's Castle is the remarkably ambitious creation of education doctoral student and Vietnam veteran Paul Gwynn. We include it here because of the wonderful array of mythological links that Gwynn has stored in the castle's armory. But this site is primarily dedicated to making history attractive to students of all ages, so we recommend it as an excellent source of historical information for interdisciplinary theme units as well.

In the mythology section of *Odin's Castle* your students can find links, for example, to *Folklore and Mythology Electronic Texts, Beowulf, Faerie Lore and Literature, Werewolf Legends from Germany, Irish Folklore, Voodoo*, and *Conan the Barbarian*. His goal is clearly to both delight and instruct as he provides access through his extensive list of links to everything "from the top of Olympus to the depths of Dr. Frankenstein's laboratory."

POETRY

A Haiku Homepage

http://home.clara.net/pka/haiku/haiku.htm	
Intended Audience	Teachers and students
Grade Level	8–12
Curricular Fit	Creative writing
Types of Resources	Links to famous haiku poets, amateur poets' contributions
Authorship of Site	Phil Adams
Navigation	Good
Visual Appeal	Fair
Interactive Activity	Visiting poets can post their haiku at this page

Phil Adams has created a page from which you and your students can explore haiku and contribute their own poems to the page. The poems at this site would be less likely to appeal to younger children than to adolescents because of their sophistication and understatement. Your students will find here a nice combination of ancient and contemporary, professional and amateur poems.

The Academy of American Poets—Online Poetry Classroom

Online Poetry Classroom, http://www.onlinepoetryclassroom.org, is a program of the Academy of American Poets (http://www.poets.org). Copyright © 2001.

http://www.onlinepoetryclassroom.org/	
Intended Audience	Teachers and students
Grade Level	9–12
Curricular Fit	American poets
Types of Resources	List of American poets and their works, audio files of poems, lesson plans
Authorship of Site	The Academy of American Poets
Navigation	Good
Visual Appeal	Fair
Interactive Activity	Listening to famous poets read their works

The *Academy of American Poets* page contains a large collection of audio files of famous authors such as Robert Frost, e. e. cummings, and T. S. Eliot reading their poems. Students can follow along with their eyes, scanning the text on the screen while they listen to the poets' interpretive readings. It is truly fascinating to be able to hear the voices of these writers. This site also provides many online lessons prepared by teachers who make use of the website's wonderful collection of American poems to teach high school students how to think about the themes expressed by famous poets and to develop their own critical and poetic skills.

Glossary of Poetic Terms

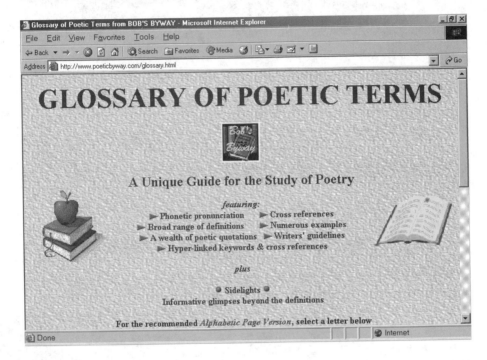

http://www.poeticbyway.com/glossary.html	
Intended Audience	Teachers and students
Grade Level	9–12
Curricular Fit	Poetry reading
Types of Resources	Hypertextually link set of poetic terms and poems
Authorship of Site	Robert G. Shubinski
Navigation	Good
Visual Appeal	Good
Interactive Activity	None

In the *Glossary of Poetic Terms* your students can study a particular poetic device by reading a definition of the term that contains links to other related terms and also provides an example from a poem. Thus they can learn that a *caesura* is a "rhythmic break or pause in the flow of *sound* which is commonly introduced in about the middle of a line of verse," and they are encouraged to follow a hyperlink to the word *sound*. A second hypertextual link takes them to the Emily Dickinson poem, "I'm Nobody! Who Are You?" which contains a caesura in its first line. This is a very effective way to enable students to learn important poetic terms.

Twentieth-Century Poetry in English

http://www.lit.kobe-u.ac.jp/~hishika/20c_poet.htm	
Intended Audience	Teachers and students
Grade Level	10–12
Curricular Fit	Modern poetry
Types of Resources	E-texts of poems, literary criticism, 170 authors' biographies
Authorship of Site	Eiichi Hishikawa
Navigation	Good
Visual Appeal	Good
Interactive Activity	None

Professor Eiichi Hishikawa of Kobe University in Japan has provided in this site special pages devoted to 11 famous poets such as W. H. Auden and William Butler Yeats. Links are included as well to 159 other twentieth-century poets. He has also inserted into his pages e-text versions of many poems by these authors and links to other interesting sites about their lives and works. Literary criticism by and about these authors is included as well as extensive bibliographies.

SHORT STORIES

Short Stories

http://www.short-stories.co.uk/	
Intended Audience	Teachers and students
Grade Level	8–12
Curricular Fit	Short stories
Types of Resources	E-texts of classic short stories
Authorship of Site	Hyperfiction
Navigation	Good
Visual Appeal	Good
Interactive Activity	None

This site contains the e-text versions of classic short stories by masters of the genre such as Edgar Allan Poe and Saki. It also contains stories by talented contemporary short story writers. Most of the classic tales are still taught in high schools and continue to entertain adolescents. Teachers have contributed to the *Short Stories* site detailed lesson plans for several of the tales and there are plans for more lessons to be added in the future. The site also contains a discussion board where readers can meet to share their interpretations of the stories.

The Moonlit Road

http://www.themoonlitroad.com/	
Intended Audience	Teachers and students
Grade Level	6–12
Curricular Fit	Short stories—supernatural and suspense
Types of Resources	Audio files and e-text of stories
Authorship of Site	The Moonlit Road Bookshop
Navigation	Good
Visual Appeal	Good
Interactive Activity	Listening to and reading ghost stories from America's South

Each month *The Moonlit Road* features ghost stories and strange folktales from the American South, which are told by the region's best storytellers. By simply selecting stories, your students can hear the storytellers recount their ghostly tales. The stories featured on this site change each month, so you may need to check to see if the particular tales that are available when you want to take your students to this site are appropriate.

NOVELS

Project Gutenberg Electronic Texts

http://promo.net/pg/history.html	
Intended Audience	University students
Grade Level	4–12
Curricular Fit	British and American literature prior to 1950
Types of Resources	E-texts of English literature classics
Authorship of Site	Michael Hart
Navigation	Good
Visual Appeal	Fair
Interactive Activity	None

Whether you want to read the electronic text of William Blake's *Songs of Innocence and Experience* or Edith Nesbit's *Five Children and It,* you can find classics of all kinds at the *Project Gutenberg* page. Begun in 1971 by Michael Hart, this project has over the years attempted to store electronic versions of many of the world's classics in English. Your students can discover here the full-text versions of hundreds of famous works, and they can navigate their way through those books by using one of the edit functions in their Netscape browser. For instance, if they want to determine how many references there are to *blood* in Shakespeare's *Macbeth,* then they can use Netscape's "find in page" function to conduct a search of Project Gutenberg's e-text version of the play.

From Robert Louis Stevenson's *A Child's Garden of Verses* to Jonathan Swift's *Gulliver's Travels,* this is the ultimate site for e-texts of the classics of English literature.

EducETH Reading List for Class Use

http://educeth.ethz.ch/english/readinglist/	
Intended Audience	Teachers and students
Grade Level	10–12
Curricular Fit	American and British literature
Types of Resources	Book summaries, lesson plans, discussion lists
Authorship of Site	Hans G. Fischer
Navigation	Good
Visual Appeal	Fair
Interactive Activity	Students can ask questions about commonly studied texts

This site contains a list of more than 70 of the most commonly studied novels in senior high school English literature classes. Everything from Chinua Achebe's *Things Fall Apart* to John Wyndham's *The Chrysalids* is included in this helpful site. If we consider one work, Alice Walker's *The Color Purple,* for example, your students can read a synopsis of the novel, biographical sketches of the author, critical commentary about the book, poems by Walker about racism, comments and questions by other students about the book, and a description of the movie directed by Stephen Spielberg that was based upon the book. This site is particularly useful for new teachers who are confronted with teaching the regular canon of senior high school literary texts for the first time and need to access some basic materials about these texts to aid them in their lesson planning. It is also of course a valuable site for students to visit who want to ask questions of other students about these texts.

A Teaching Unit for Treasure Island

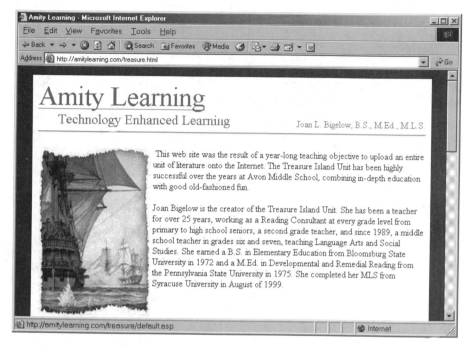

Amity Learning LLC

http://amitylearning.com/treasure.html	
Intended Audience	Teachers and students
Grade Level	6–9
Curricular Fit	Novel study and pirate theme unit
Types of Resources	Questions about pirates, map, puppet show ideas
Authorship of Site	Joan Bigelow
Navigation	Good
Visual Appeal	Good
Interactive Activity	Constructing a Jolly Roger, researching a pirate, etc.

In this fun-filled site students carry out in-depth research on a pirate or a topic related to pirates, learn 30 or more basic parts of a schooner, hear treachery from within an apple barrel, design a personal Jolly Roger, bury treasure sought by ten surly pirates, eat limes and lemons to prevent scurvy, and discover a skeleton pointing the way to a fortune in gold, silver, and jewels. In other words, they have a good deal of fun absorbing knowledge connected with the classic novel *Treasure Island*.

F. Scott Fitzgerald Centenary

http://www.sc.edu/fitzgerald/index.html	
Intended Audience	Students and teachers
Grade Level	11–12
Curricular Fit	American literature
Types of Resources	Biography, bibliography of works by and about Fitzgerald
Authorship of Site	Board of Trustees of the University of South Carolina
Navigation	Good
Visual Appeal	Good
Interactive Activity	Audio and video clips of Fitzgerald

This site and the *Treasure Island* page are examples of rich resources about one or a few novels of particular authors. If you perform a web search using *Yahoo, Google,* and other search engines, you can sometimes find sites of this sort by simply typing in the title of the work or the name of the author. In the case of the *F. Scott Fitzgerald Centenary* site, your students will discover a biography of Fitzgerald, a bibliography of works by and about him, several lengthy essays that discuss his novels, audio files of Fitzgerald reading poetry by Keats, Masefield, and Shakespeare, and a video clip of the author in the 1920s. The University of North Carolina has also provided famous quotes by Fitzgerald and facts about the author that provide readers with glimpses, for instance, into his relationship with Hemingway.

DRAMA

Readers Theatre Edition

http://www.aaronshep.com/rt/RTE.html	
Intended Audience	Teachers and students
Grade Level	K–6
Curricular Fit	Drama in the English Language Arts classroom
Types of Resources	Scripts for elementary students
Authorship of Site	Aaron Shepard
Navigation	Good
Visual Appeal	Fair
Interactive Activity	33 free scripts for immediate use

Award-winning children's author Aaron Sheppard has developed this site that contains 33 of his free, K–6 *Readers Theatre* scripts for immediate use. These humorous texts provide a pleasurable vehicle for improving your students' oral reading and interpretation skills.

The Improv Page

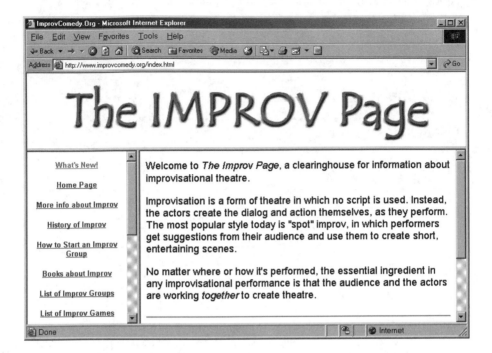

http://www.improvcomedy.org/index.html	
Intended Audience	Teachers and students
Grade Level	K–12
Curricular Fit	Drama in the English and Theater Arts classroom
Types of Resources	Many teaching ideas for improvisation activities
Authorship of Site	Bernie Roehl
Navigation	Good
Visual Appeal	Fair
Interactive Activity	None at the computer but much in the English classroom

It is not always essential for English language arts sites to involve on-screen interactivity. In *The Improv Page,* for example, you will find no audio or video clips, nor will you even find any pictures or animations. But the words at this site provide excellent opportunities for students to interact with texts, with fellow actors, and with their audience in wonderfully imaginative ways. Besides providing links to sites about improv artists, information about the history of improvisation, and a list of improv terms, this site contains links to lists of well over 300 different improv games and activities for your students to enjoy. For instance, in a game titled Dubbing, off-stage improvisers provide the voices for the onstage characters and action. This activity may also be performed as a foreign film. Or, in another variation, the voice players do not watch the scene and therefore may contradict it. The body players must physically justify what they are saying.

The Dramatic Exchange Catalogue of Plays

http://www.dramex.org/index.shtml	
Intended Audience	Teachers and students
Grade Level	K–12
Curricular Fit	Drama in the English and Theater Arts classroom
Types of Resources	E-texts of more than 300 plays
Authorship of Site	Mike Dederian and Rob Knop
Navigation	Good
Visual Appeal	Fair
Interactive Activity	Reading plays

Many English and drama teachers have been in the difficult position of attempting to find an appropriate play to use with their English or theater arts classes or in a school Drama Club production. Unfortunately, the one-paragraph descriptions found in traditional sources of plays, such as the *Samuel French Catalogue,* do not provide enough information about the plays to indicate clearly whether or not they will prove suitable. At the *Dramatic Exchange* site, instead of trying to guess about the quality of a play through a single paragraph, you can find both a short description and the entire text of more than 300 contemporary plays. The plays are organized according to the following categories: comedies, tragedies, mysteries, dramas, one-acts, full-length plays, musicals, children's theater, plays for screen, audience participation, and experimental plays. At the *Dramatic Exchange* you can skim through entire plays until you find the ones you want.

The Puppetry Homepage

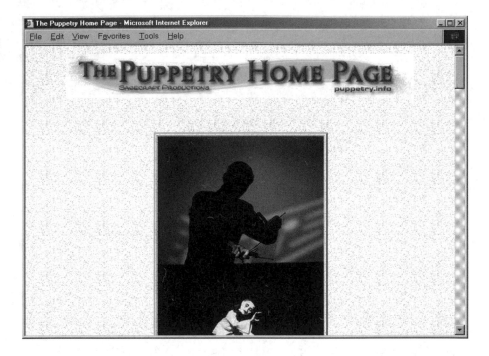

http://www.sagecraft.com/puppetry/	
Intended Audience	Teachers and students
Grade Level	K–12
Curricular Fit	Puppets may be used in any Language Arts course
Types of Resources	Definitions, traditions, museums, performances
Authorship of Site	Sagecraft Productions
Navigation	Good
Visual Appeal	Good
Interactive Activity	Students can build their own puppets and perform plays

At this beautifully illustrated site you and your students can learn about puppetry organizations, festivals, and theatres. You can study definitions, worldwide traditions, and schools of puppetry. You can also visit exhibits and museums about puppetry. You can learn how to build puppets, and you can find out about various performance companies, sites, and resources. With the help of this web, you and your students can build your own puppets and perform plays in a number of different styles and traditions such as the Balinese shadow puppets, Japanese Bunraku puppets, and English Punch and Judy puppets. This site is truly a feast for the imagination.

The WWW Virtual Library of Theatre and Drama

http://vl-theatre.com/	
Intended Audience	Teachers and students
Grade Level	6–12
Curricular Fit	Drama in the English and Theater Arts classrooms
Types of Resources	E-texts of plays, articles, museums, theatre images
Authorship of Site	WWW Virtual Library
Navigation	Good
Visual Appeal	Good
Interactive Activity	Fair

This site contains a vast range of links to international online plays, articles, journals, museums, organizations, and collections of theatre images. Its multicultural and multilingual resources have been gathered from more than 50 countries around the world. If, for instance, you are planning to stage a Greek or medieval play in your class, or if you are teaching one of Moliere's comedies, you can find the information you need at this rich site.

BRITISH AUTHORS

British and Irish Authors on the Web

http://lang.nagoya-u.ac.jp/~matsuoka/UK-authors.html

The *British and Irish Authors on the Web* site lists authors chronologically from the year AD 600 to the present. The site itself contains only a list of hyperlinks to other sites, but what a list! From its first site on *Beowulf,* where your students can read *Beowulf* in the original Old English or do a word search in a modern English translation, to one of the most recent entries (as of this writing), where they can learn about some of Kazuo Ishiguro's works such as his Booker Prize–winning novel, *The Remains of the Day,* your students have literally hundreds of wonderful British and Irish authors' sites to choose from.

The Shakespeare Resource Center

http://www.bardweb.net/

This site deals not only with Shakespeare's literature, but also with Shakespeare as a man and the environment in which he lived and wrote. It has a built-in search tool to help your students find information about Shakespeare's life and works more easily. By referring to the link on the authorship debate, students may read about other Elizabethan authors, such as Christopher Marlowe and Francis Bacon, in order to consider the validity of arguments about whether or not all of the plays attributed to Shakespeare were actually written by him. As well, they can learn about the nuances of Elizabethan English.

Mr. William Shakespeare and the Internet

http://shakespeare.palomar.edu/

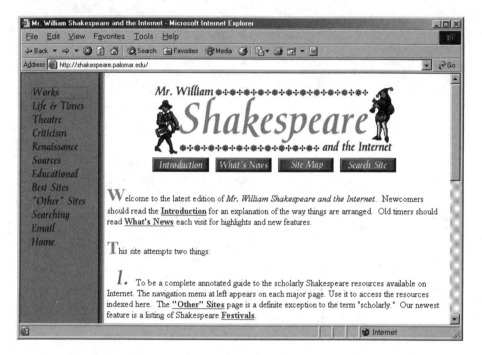

This site contains study notes for most of Shakespeare's plays as well as many other useful features. For example, you may take a virtual tour through the Globe theatre, learn about Elizabethan music, read all of the plays online, visit Shakespeare's birthplace in Stratford, follow links to many other educational sites, read study guides and literary criticism for the plays.

The Brontë Sisters Web

http://lang.nagoya-u.ac.jp/~matsuoka/Bronte.html

Among the e-texts available at the *Brontë Sisters Web* site are the novels *Jane Eyre* by Charlotte and *Wuthering Heights* by Emily. If you are planning to have your students read either of these novels, it is likely that you have provided them with a paperback version. Nevertheless, when they wish to do research into the appearance of certain important words in these novels, by performing a simple electronic word search they can easily discover for themselves, for instance, that there are more than 100 references to the word "fire" in *Jane Eyre*. As well as studying the novels of the

Brontë sisters, here your students can read poems by Charlotte, Emily, and Anne or they can study a fascinating book-length biography of Charlotte published in 1857, just two years after her death, by her friend, Mrs. Elizabeth Gaskell. There are also many other excellent resources on this page, such as a painting of the Brontës and a photograph of the parsonage where they grew up.

The Dickens Page

http://lang.nagoya-u.ac.jp/~matsuoka/Dickens.html

From the Dickens home page your students can access e-texts of several of Charles Dickens' books such as *Great Expectations* and *Oliver Twist.* They can also hear readings by an actor of short passages from *A Christmas Carol,* and they can read an e-text book-length biography of Dickens written in 1874 by his friend, John Forster. A concordance, bibliography, and message board are here as well. If you would like to order a film version of one of his books, the Dickens Filmography lists more than 80 films.

Sherlockian.Net

http://www.sherlockian.net/

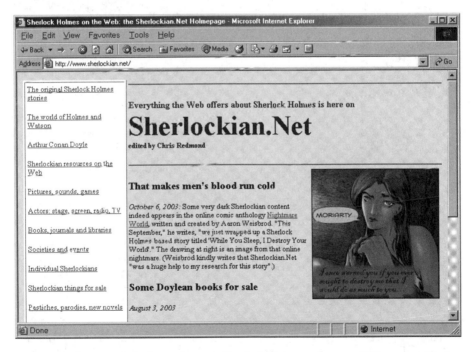

Reputed to be one of the best of many *Sherlock Holmes* pages on the Internet, Chris Redmond's *Sherlockian.Net* contains links to hundreds of other Holmes pages that your students can visit. For example, through these links they can take a virtual tour of the Sherlock Holmes Museum, where they will see some of the items that are on display at 221b Baker Street, such as Sherlock Holmes's Stradivarius violin and Dr. Watson's diary. Or they can read the biography of Sir Arthur Conan Doyle, which contains hyperlinks to information on Spiritualism and Ghosts on Film. They may read any of the *Sherlock Holmes* stories in e-text form, and they can view the original artwork accompanying these stories when they were first published. If they wish, students may listen to an actor's rendition of Holmes's lines, such as Sir Ralph Richardson stating that Professor Moriarty "is the Napoleon of crime. He is the organizer of half that is evil and of nearly all that is undetected in this great city." Truly committed Holmes fans may even wish to join one of the Sherlock Holmes societies around the world or to learn about the many stage, screen, television, and radio versions of the Sherlock Holmes stories. They may even read about the lives of actors, such as Basil Rathbone and Jeremy Brett, who have made Holmes so popular in film and television portrayals of the great detective.

Into the Wardrobe: A Web Site Devoted to C. S. Lewis

http://cslewis.drzeus.net/

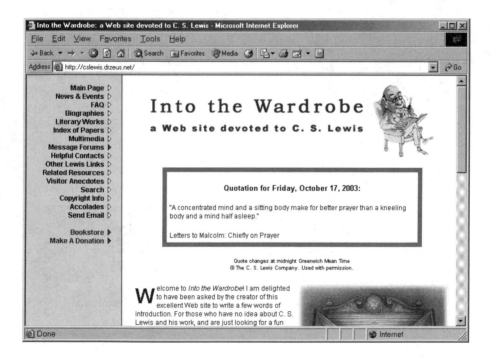

Because the works of C. S. Lewis, such as *The Chronicles of Narnia,* are still protected by copyright, they are not yet available in e-text versions. Nevertheless, this site contains a very good annotated bibliography to help uninitiated readers determine which of Lewis's books they might wish to read. It even recommends the proper order in which to read the Narnia books. The site also contains interesting bio-graphical essays and articles about Lewis's novels such as Matt Brennan's "The Lion, The Witch, and the Allegory: An Analysis of Selected Narnia Chronicles." Students may view here as well a map of Narnia and various beautiful images such as a paint-ing of Aslan the lion. Finally, many audio clips are included of Lewis and others reading from his works.

George Orwell Homepage

http://www.k-1.com/Orwell/

If you are teaching *1984* or *Animal Farm,* you might find the interpretations of these novels that are provided on the *George Orwell Homepage* to be useful. The complete text of Orwell's essay, "Politics and the English Language," is available here and is a useful tool with which to help your students analyze the propaganda techniques practiced by Big Brother and Napoleon the pig in Orwell's novels. Your students might also find the biography of Orwell and some of his other essays to be useful in understanding his novels, and they might enjoy learning about some of Orwell's other books, such as *Burmese Days* and *Homage to Catalonia.* If they wish to share their ideas about his works they may join the Orwell Discussion Board.

AMERICAN AUTHORS

American Authors on the Web

http://lang.nagoya-u.ac.jp/~matsuoka/AmeLit.html

This amazing list of resources contains more than 1,000 links to information on American authors, from the popular contemporary writers such as Tom Clancy and Amy Tan, to the traditionally revered authors such as Edgar Allan Poe, Emily Dick-inson, and Mark Twain. It is definitely a good place to begin your search for teach-ing ideas about American authors.

Literary Resources—American

http://andromeda.rutgers.edu/~jlynch/Lit/american.html

While this list of resources contains fewer links than the preceding one (less than 200), it differs from *American Authors on the Web* in that, as well as providing an ex-cellent selection of author homepages, it also offers links to a number of overview sites, with titles such as *19th Century American Women Writers, The Mississippi Writers' Page,* and *Native American Literature Online.* At the *Beat* poetry site, *Literary Kicks,* for instance, senior high school students can study the work of Jack Kerouac, Allen Ginsberg, and Lawrence Ferlinghetti. Or, if they visit the jazz literature archive site, *Epistrophy,* they will encounter an impressive collection of writings on literature and jazz, with introductions, samples of jazz fiction and poetry, and essays.

Edgar Allan Poe's House of Usher

http://www.comnet.ca/~forrest/

When your students first arrive at this delightfully macabre multimedia site they will encounter morbid, spine-tingling music and a bloodcurdling scream! They can then read a brief biography of Poe and, by visiting *The Poe Decoder* site, study some very helpful interpretations of his work. If they wish to see some of the houses where Poe and his 13-year-old wife lived, they can follow the *Poe's Favorite Haunts* link. If they wish to read e-texts of his works or study criticism about "The Black Cat," "The Raven," and many other stories and poems by Poe, they can proceed to *The Poe Virtual Library.* In the pages devoted to Poe's recurrent motifs and themes, your students will encounter animations of a beating heart and gnashing teeth. Through the *Edgar Allan Poe Theatre's* Real Audio feed they can listen to dramatizations of stories such as "The Mask of the Red Death." All these imaginative features will undoubtedly delight many adolescent visitors.

The Road Not Taken: Robert Frost's Lesser Known Poems

http://frost.freehosting.net/index.htm

At this site your students can read Frost's well-known poems such as "Mending Wall" and "The Road Not Taken," but they can also read some of his lesser-known poems. Resources such as essays about the poems, biographical information, links to other sites, and photographs make this one of the most attractive and informative Frost sites on the Internet.

The Hemingway Resource Center

http://www.lostgeneration.com

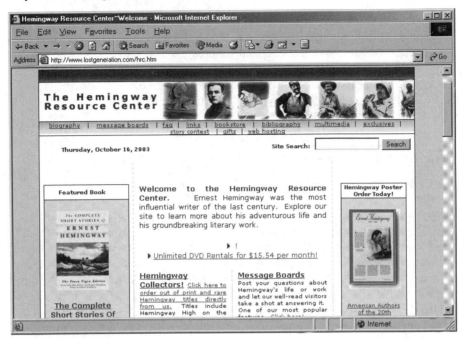

At the *Hemingway Resource Center* your students can find many photographs of Ernest Hemingway taken during his years as a writer, soldier, and hunter. Students can read answers to a list of FAQs about the author such as, "What characterizes Hemingway's writing style?" and they can listen to an audio file of Hemingway reading his Nobel Prize acceptance speech. Also available at this site are an illustrated six-part biography of Hemingway and a bibliography of books by and about Hemingway. Some of the many links that this site provides to other Hemingway pages are *Hemingway's Birthplace, The Running of the Bulls,* and *The Hemingway Cookbook.*

John Steinbeck Page

http://ocean.st.usm.edu/~wsimkins/steinb.html

A few of John Steinbeck's writings are available through this site, such as his essays from America and Americans and a selection of his letters from *Steinbeck: A Life in Letters.* But the most valuable feature of this site for teachers and students of Steinbeck's work is an extensive annotated bibliography of criticism written about his books. One of the related sites to which this one is linked is the *Of Mice and Men Student Survival Guide,* which provides hyperlinked definitions of words, references for allusions, and explanations of idioms for each chapter of this popular Steinbeck novel.

The Mississippi Writers Page: Tennessee Williams

http://www.olemiss.edu/depts/english/ms-writers/dir/williams_tennessee/

At this Tennessee Williams site your students may view a number of photographs of Williams at various stages in his career. This web page also contains a biography of Tennessee Williams as well as excellent summaries of a few of his more famous plays, such as *A Streetcar Named Desire*. One of this site's related links will take your students to a page devoted to Williams' play *The Glass Menagerie*, where they can read biographical, feminist, and psychoanalytic critical analyses, listen to audio clips, and view video clips of the play.

Crucible Homepage

http://www.geocities.com/CollegePark/Classroom/3085/crucible.html

There are many excellent links from this site to specific aspects of Arthur Miller's play, *The Crucible*. The first link takes you to *A Teacher's Cyberguide* for the play, which contains interesting teaching activities. For instance, students are asked to write a persuasive letter to the governor of Salem calling for action against the trials or to compose a tribute to the accused. They learn about the setting and the historical background of *The Crucible* and take a web tour of historical Salem, including a visit to the Witch Trials Memorial. They also read a chronology of the historical events of the witch trials. Another interesting link from *The Crucible* page provides an audio clip of the anti-Communist American Senator Joe McCarthy, the person upon whom Miller based the character of Danforth.

Anniina's Amy Tan Page

http://www.luminarium.org/contemporary/amytan/

Amy Tan's homepage contains an illustrated version of one of her short stories, numerous reviews of her novels, and an enchanting audio clip of her account about her fascination with ghosts and with the enduring power of love. It also contains several biographical sketches of Amy Tan and links to a number of interesting essays with titles such as "Chinese-American Women in American Culture."

CANADIAN AUTHORS

Northwest Passages: Canadian Literature On-Line

http://www.nwpassages.com/links.asp

This encyclopedic site connects to more than 200 Canadian authors' pages. It also contains many excellent links to web sites on Canadian literature, publishers, periodicals, organizations, programs, and associations. It provides an extensive set of links to sites on African Canadian literature, British Columbian fiction writers, Canadian children's books, Canadian science fiction, the Canadian literature discussion group, winners of the Stephen Leacock Medal for Humor, and women in Canadian literature as well.

Margaret Atwood Information Site

http://www.cariboo.bc.ca/atwood/

The Atwood Society has created this *Margaret Atwood Information Site* to display for interested scholars lists of Atwood's novels, books of poetry, short stories, criticism, children's books, interviews, films, sound recordings, and dramatic works. This site also contains an extensive list of books about Margaret Atwood's life and works, such as the collection of essays titled *Approaches to Teaching Margaret Atwood's Handmaid's Tale and Other Works.* Among the Internet resources listed at this site is Margaret Atwood's own homepage. The Atwood Society's page, however, is more extensive than Atwood's own site, so it is still the best place to start your search for resources on one of Canada's leading contemporary writers.

Michael Ondaatje Information

http://www.cariboo.bc.ca/ae/engml/FRIEDMAN/ondaatje.htm

Since the movie *The English Patient* won so many Academy Awards, most high school students will be familiar with the film based upon Michael Ondaatje's Booker Prize–winning novel. At this site they can learn more about the movie and book, the author's biography, and his other novels. One particularly valuable feature of this site is its lengthy and detailed index of words and phrases from *The English Patient,* which could prove useful to senior high school students should you choose to teach them the novel.

MULTICULTURAL AND WORLD LITERATURE AUTHORS

Native American Authors

http://www.ipl.org/ref/native/

For students and teachers who would like to discover information about Canadian and American First Nations authors, the *Native American Authors* site contains a list of 400 writers in which can be found brief biographies and detailed catalogues of the 700 books they have written. Here students can read, for example, about the lives and works of Canadian First Nations writers such as Rita Joe, Tomson Highway, and Ruby Slipperjack, or American First Nations authors N. Scott Momaday, James Welch, and Paula Gunn Allen.

The Index of Native American Electronic Text Resources

http://www.hanksville.org/NAresources/indices/NAetext.html

The *Index of Native American Electronic Text Resources* on the Internet contains many contemporary and historical essays, poems, and short stories by Canadian and American writers. For instance, Thomas King's essay, "Shooting the Lone Ranger," and Leslie Marmon Silko's essay, "Fences Against Freedom," are available online through this extensive index.

Literary Resources—Other National Literatures

http://andromeda.rutgers.edu/~jlynch/Lit/other.html

Some of the many countries whose literatures are represented on this site in English or English translation are Australia, New Zealand, France, Germany, India, Ireland, Italy, Japan, Spain, and Turkey. Through the link to South Asian Women's Literature, for example, your students can learn about the lives and works of such famous South Asian writers as Anita Desai, Ruth Prawar Jhabvala, and Mahasweta Devi. Or, through the Literature of South Asia and the Indian Diaspora site, they can explore a large assortment of links to learn about the works of writers such as Salman Rushdie, Rohinton Mistry, and R. K. Narayan.

Kazuo Ishiguro

http://www.cyberartsweb.org/post/uk/ishiguro/ishiguroov.html

George P. Landow, *Postcolonial Literature and Culture Web*

Kazuo Ishiguro moved to England when he was six years old and grew up straddling two societies, the Japan of his parents and his adopted England. This site about the author of the award-winning novels *The Remains of the Day* and *Pale View of Hills* contains many interesting essays about Ishiguro's narrative technique, his themes of honesty and deception, his use of language and imagery, and many other topics.

SUGGESTED ACTIVITIES

1. Visit the *Children's Literature Web Guide* and some of the other major children's literature sites that are linked to it, such as Carol Hurst's site and Kay Vandergrift's. With your school librarian and/or your fellow language arts teachers, select a number of author pages and then construct theme units around clusters of their works. For instance, under the theme of "perilous journeys" you could include sites about the *Wizard of Oz* and *Alice in Wonderland.*

2. Encourage your adolescent students to visit the sites of authors whose works they have been studying, such as Gary Paulsen or S. E. Hinton, and to report to the class what they have learned about the authors' biographies and related works. If a particular site provides an opportunity to contact the author, they could also be encouraged to send an e-mail in which they ask questions about the author's life and works.

3. For students who have an interest in science fiction, you could ask them to visit a site about one of their favorite authors and do one of the following: (1) read a few of the linked essays about the author's books and write a brief summary of their main arguments, or (2) view and critique some of the artwork inspired by the author's books and then draw their own picture based upon one of their favorite scenes.

4. While your students are reading stories from several mythology sites, encourage them to compare the archetypal patterns in myths from different cultures (heroes, quests, monsters, morals, etc.).

5. Have your students select and print out from different sites a number of their favorite poems (written by students or professional authors) about a common theme such as love or the seasons, then write, illustrate, and record one of their own poems about the same theme. Finally, have them post their poem on an Internet site such as Poetry Pals.

6. Find a lesson plan from a site such as EducETH about a novel which you teach and adapt that plan to suit the needs of your students.

7. In connection with a theme your students are studying, encourage them to visit the Improv Page and to perform several of the improvisations described at this site. Or download scripts from the Dramatic Exchange site that deal with this theme and have your students perform them.

8. From the assortment of British, American, Canadian, multicultural, and world literature author sites provided in this chapter, have each of your secondary school students select a different author for an independent study project.

SUMMARY

In this chapter we have introduced you to a wide range of literature sites that contain, for example, critical essays, audio clips of poetry readings, author biographies, and interactive lesson plans. Artwork, student writing, and film critiques are also included here. All of these resources can expand your repertoire beyond the usual options for teaching literature appreciation. Even though we have barely scratched the surface, we hope that this chapter has helped you to recognize the potential of these literature sites.

CHAPTER 5

Language Arts Standards and Activities

- English Language Arts Standards
- Researching the History of English Literature
- Grammar Online
- Publishing and Exploring Student Writing
- Writing for Newspapers and Magazines
- Debating and Speech Writing
- Composing and Sharing Multimedia Presentations
- English-as-a-Second-Language (ESL) Projects and Resources
- Intercultural Communication Via E-mail
- Comparing Other Languages with English
- Creating School Homepages
- Newspapers and Magazines

ENGLISH LANGUAGE ARTS STANDARDS

In 1996 the International Reading Association (IRA) and the National Council of Teachers of English (NCTE) established a set of standards for the study of English in their document, *Standards for the English Language Arts* (**http://www.ncte.org/ standards/thelist.html**). In this chapter we have identified a number of sites you may find useful for enabling your students to achieve these various literacy standards. For instance, one of the NCTE standards is for students to be able to "read a wide range of print and nonprint texts to build an understanding of texts, of themselves, and of the cultures of the United States and the world." To help your students to develop their print and media literacy skills, therefore, we have described how you can use a number of newspaper, magazine, and film sites to show your students how to understand events and ideas in their country and their world.

Another important NCTE standard is for your students to be able to "read a wide range of literature from many periods in many genres to build an understanding of the many dimensions of human experience." At the end of the previous chapter we showed you some of the splendid multicultural and world literature sites available for elementary and secondary school students to visit, but in this chapter we also present some Internet pages that are devoted to the history of English literature so that you can aid young readers to view human experience through the eyes of some of England's finest writers. A related standard is to be able to "apply a wide range of strategies to comprehend, interpret, evaluate, and appreciate texts," so in this section on researching the history of English literature, we begin by providing you with an excellent literary criticism site.

Three standards that concern how to teach students to become more effective writers are to "adjust their use of spoken, written, and visual language to communicate effectively with a variety of audiences and for different purposes, to employ a wide range of strategies as they write and use different writing process elements appropriately to communicate with different audiences for a variety of purposes, and to participate as knowledgeable, reflective, creative, and critical members of a variety of literacy communities." So that you may enable your students to achieve these three standards, we provide a number of sites under the headings of "Publishing and Exploring Student Writing" and "Writing for Newspapers and Magazines" that show how to write well and how to publish work on the Internet.

Concerning your students' need to be able to "apply knowledge of language structure, language conventions, media techniques, figurative language, and genre to create, critique, and discuss print and nonprint texts," we have brought together in this chapter a number of pages devoted to helping your students with grammar and to showing them how to compose and share multimedia presentations. And our sections on intercultural communication via email, comparing other languages with English, and creating school homepages will help your students to realize their potential to "(1) conduct research on issues and interests by generating ideas and questions and by posing problems; (2) develop an understanding and respect for diversity and language use, patterns, and dialects across cultures, ethnic groups, geographic regions, and social roles; and (3) use a variety of technological and informational resources to gather and synthesize information to create and communicate knowledge."

Finally, in this chapter we have selected some very good ESL project and resource pages to help your elementary and secondary school ESL students achieve the NCTE standard of "making use of their first language to develop competency in English language arts and develop understanding across the curriculum." And for all your students who need to learn how to "use spoken, written, and visual language to accomplish their own purposes (learning, enjoyment, persuasion, and exchange of information," the debating and speech writing sites assembled here should help them to improve their powers of persuasion in speaking and writing.

In this chapter, then, we ask you to bear in mind these NCTE standards for the study of English language arts so that you can see how particular sites may help you to guide your students toward the achievement of each of the learning outcomes just delineated.

RESEARCHING THE HISTORY OF ENGLISH LITERATURE

When you are teaching students about the history of English literature, the following sites will enable you to show them the writings of different authors over the centuries. The first site provides an overview of British and American literature and literary criticism from the fourteenth century to the present. The subsequent sites enable you to focus on particular eras by viewing original manuscripts and listening to audio clips of the works of Chaucer and others.

Online Literary Criticism Collection

http://www.ipl.org/div/litcrit/	
Intended Audience	Students and teachers
Grade Level	9–12
Curricular Fit	English language study and Old English literature
Types of Resources	Lists of literary criticism and author websites
Authorship of Site	The Internet Public Library
Navigation	Good
Visual Appeal	Good
Interactive Activity	None

The *Online Literary Criticism Collection* site provides an incredibly large collection of links to sites such as *The English Language in the Fourteenth Century,* which describes the changes that took place in the English language during the fourteenth century by focusing particularly upon the language used in *The Canterbury Tales* and how that reflected the dialects of Chaucer's times. As well as critical and linguistic sites, this page can connect you to homepages and biographical information about many of the most famous British and American writers.

Labyrinth Library: Middle English Bookcase

http://www.georgetown.edu/labyrinth/library/me/me.html	
Intended Audience	Students and teachers
Grade Level	9–12
Curricular Fit	English language study and Middle English literature
Types of Resources	Electronic texts of Chaucer's Canterbury Tales and others
Authorship of Site	Martin Irvine and Deborah Everhart at Georgetown University
Navigation	Good
Visual Appeal	Good
Interactive Activity	None

This site contains the complete texts of many famous Middle English works such as *Sir Gawain and the Green Knight, Everyman, The Vision of Piers Plowman,* and *The Canterbury Tales.* It also has links to other anthologies and collections of Medieval literature in which students can hear Middle English being spoken.

Renaissance Editions

http://darkwing.uoregon.edu/~rbear/	
Intended Audience	Student and teachers
Grade Level	11–12
Curricular Fit	English language study and Renaissance English literature
Types of Resources	Electronic texts, discussion list archive, critical essays
Authorship of Site	Richard Bear at the University of Oregon
Navigation	Good
Visual Appeal	Good
Interactive Activity	Some if students choose to join discussion list

The works of approximately 100 British authors between 1477 and 1799 such as Edmund Spenser, Daniel Defoe, and Jonathan Swift are available at this rich site.

The Milton-L Homepage

http://www.urich.edu/~creamer/milton/	
Intended Audience	Students, teachers, and professors
Grade Level	11–12
Curricular Fit	English language study and 17th-century English literature
Types of Resources	Essays, e-texts, audio clips of poetry, discussion lists
Authorship of Site	
Navigation	Good
Visual Appeal	Excellent
Interactive Activity	Viewing paintings and listening to poetry

The complete electronic text of Milton's *Paradise Lost* is available through this site, as are audio files of the arguments for each of the 12 books of that famous epic poem. Students can study *A John Milton Chronology,* view wonderful illustrations of his poetry, and read reviews of recently published books about the life and works of Milton.

Luminarium: Medieval, Renaissance, and 17th-Century Literary Anthologies

http://www.luminarium.org/

Intended Audience	Students and teachers
Grade Level	9–12
Curricular Fit	English language study, 15th- through 17th-century literature
Types of Resources	Paintings, music and poetry audio files, e-texts, critical essays
Authorship of Site	Luminarium
Navigation	Good
Visual Appeal	Excellent
Interactive Activity	Listening to poetry and music and viewing illustrations

At the *Luminarium Medieval, Renaissance, and 17th Century English Literature* sites, your students can study ancient manuscripts, listen to portions of Chaucer's *Canterbury Tales* being read, or view the original title page of Christopher Marlowe's *Dr. Faustus.* There is a wonderful collection of essays at each site with which your students could carry out independent study projects. The sites' index pages even provide medieval and Renaissance music clips for your students' listening pleasure. This is an exceptionally well-presented and interesting set of sites.

GRAMMAR ONLINE

Guide to Grammar and Writing

http://webster.commnet.edu/grammar/index.htm	
Intended Audience	Students
Grade Level	7–12
Curricular Fit	Grammar and writing process
Types of Resources	Descriptions of sentence, paragraph, and essay types
Authorship of Site	Charles Darling
Navigation	Good
Visual Appeal	Good
Interactive Activity	Questions can be asked of Gramma(r) English

At the *Guide to Grammar and Writing* site, information is available about sentence, paragraph, and essay forms. Your students can ask Gramma(r) English in her rocking chair questions about a particular grammar problem they are having. There are also several other interesting features to this site, such as the humorous grammar errors listed in the *Anomalous Anonymies* page. Some of the other activities listed here include

- Models for communication
- Interactive quizzes
- Grammar logs
- Eminent quotables
- Other online resources for writing

PUBLISHING AND EXPLORING STUDENT WRITING

In the following sites you will see opportunities to read and publish student work as well as aids to the writing process. We suggest that as well as considering these sites as venues for your students' work, you consider publishing their poems and short stories on your school's homepage so that when children and teachers from other schools come to your school's site they will quickly derive a sense of the people and place they are visiting.

Roget's Thesaurus

http://thesaurus.reference.com/	
Intended Audience	Teachers and students
Grade Level	3–12
Curricular Fit	Writing process
Types of Resources	Word search for synonyms
Authorship of Site	Lexico Publishing Group
Navigation	Good
Visual Appeal	Fair
Interactive Activity	Limited to the usual thesaurus functions

If your students are looking for just the right word to use in their poems and short stories, this site offers them an excellent opportunity to search *Roget's Thesaurus* for an extensive set of synonyms. Another site young wordsmiths should visit is *The Semantic Rhyming Dictionary* (**http://www.rhymezone.com/**).

The Biography Writer's Workshop

http://teacher.scholastic.com/writewit/biograph/	
Intended Audience	Students
Grade Level	4–12
Curricular Fit	Biographical writing in theme units
Types of Resources	Biography of Frederick Douglass, lesson plans for teachers, biography writing guide for students
Authorship of Site	Patricia and Fredrick McKissak
Navigation	Good
Visual Appeal	Good
Interactive Activity	Students can publish biographies online and read other students' biographies

This very helpful site gives students all the tools they need in order to write interesting biographies. The students are encouraged to begin by raising important questions about the person they are studying. Then they are asked to research information about that person. Finally, they are shown how to synthesize their material and organize their writing so that they can tell a good story. Samples of other students' biographical writing are provided and students receive a certificate once they have published their own work at the *Biography Writer's Workshop* site.

The Eclectic Writer

http://www.eclectics.com/writing/writing.html	
Intended Audience	Students
Grade Level	10–12
Curricular Fit	Writer's workshop
Types of Resources	Essays about writing
Authorship of Site	Eclectic InterNetWork
Navigation	Good
Visual Appeal	Good
Interactive Activity	Mainly a valuable resource page

Although this site was created with adult authors in mind, it can serve equally well as a resource for serious adolescent authors in writing courses or in your high school's writing club. *The Eclectic Writer* contains an extensive list of sites organized under the following categories:

- Web-based discussion board for writers
- Articles about writing
- Fiction writers' character chart
- Crime writing
- Romance writing
- Horror writing
- Children's writing
- Technical writing
- Screen writing
- Science fiction/fantasy writing
- Mystery writing
- Poetry
- Newsgroups
- Research
- General writing resources
- Just for fun

WRITING FOR NEWSPAPERS AND MAGAZINES

The Write Site

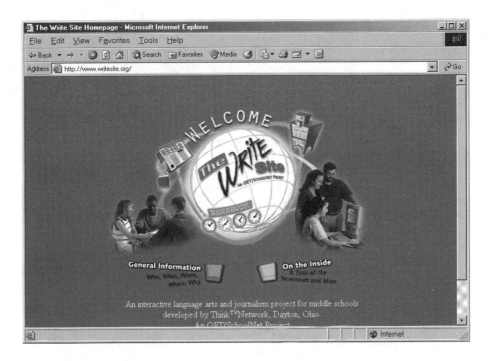

http://www.writesite.org/	
Intended Audience	Teachers and students
Grade Level	6–8
Curricular Fit	Creative writing and journalism
Types of Resources	Contains many newspaper writing resources and units
Authorship of Site	Greater Dayton Public Television
Navigation	Good
Visual Appeal	Good
Interactive Activity	Some related sites such as CNN provide video and audio

As the authors of *The Write Site* point out, middle school students who visit this multimedia language arts web page can learn how to enjoy the art of telling stories. Students assume the roles of journalists who generate leads, gather facts, and write stories by using the tools and techniques of professional journalists. Within *The Write Site's Newsroom Page for Students* are sections containing valuable links to help students write their stories.

The *Features Desk* contains links to

- The Story of Journalism in the United States
- Creating Human Interest
- Tapping News Organizations
- Cool Sites for Kids

The *Research Beat* links include

- How to Do Research
- Finding Data on the Internet
- Museums and Online Libraries

And the *Style Section* links include

- Developing Your Style
- Keeping a Journal
- Writers' Thoughts on Writing

For teachers, *The Write Site* contains four units of activities to be done with students:

- How the Newspaper Works
- A Day in the Life of a Reporter
- Newspapers in Cyberspace
- Let the Pictures Tell the Story

The Global Schoolhouse

http://www.gsn.org/	
Intended Audience	Teachers and Students
Grade Level	4–12
Curricular Fit	Writing across the curriculum
Types of Resources	Global current events by students
Authorship of Site	Global SchoolNet
Navigation	Good
Visual Appeal	Good
Interactive Activity	Opportunities to showcase your students' work globally

Like *The Write Site, The Global Schoolhouse* provides opportunities for your students to research, write, and share their stories with other students on the Internet. Your students can research stories, read articles and editorials about current world events written by young people around the globe, and share individual or class projects with other visitors to this *Global Schoolhouse* site. More than 1000 wonderful projects are listed at the site. You can take part in a current project or read the results of projects from previous years. A few of the activities your students can become involved in include: (1) following explorers as they travel to interesting locations, (2) create newspapers with the help of student correspondents in other countries, and (3) take part in video conferences with other classes around the world.

DEBATING AND SPEECH WRITING

Gifts of Speech

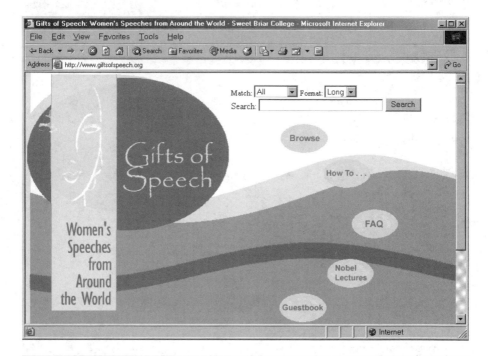

http://www.giftsofspeech.org	
Intended Audience	Students
Grade Level	10–12
Curricular Fit	Arguing from a position in written and spoken forms
Types of Resources	Large archive of famous women's speeches
Authorship of Site	Liz Kent
Navigation	Good
Visual Appeal	Good
Interactive Activity	None

Although there are many sites on the Internet devoted to debating and speech writing, if you are looking for a repository of wonderful model speeches by famous women, then the *Gifts of Speech* site is the best place to start. Among the many speeches available at this site are the 1991 Nobel Lecture on "Writing and Being" by South African writer Nadine Gordimer and the speech on "The Problem of Racism on the Threshold of the 21st Century" by Guatemalan human rights activist, Rigoberta Menchu Tum.

Virtual Presentation Assistant

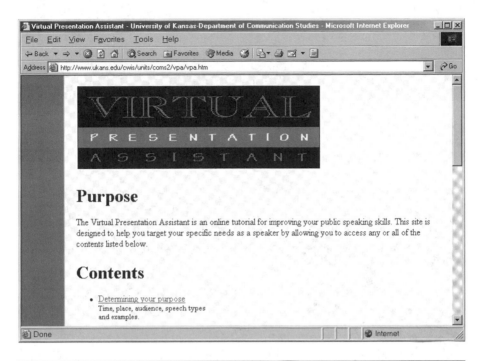

http://www.ukans.edu/cwis/units/coms2/vpa/vpa.htm	
Intended Audience	Students and teachers
Grade Level	8–12
Curricular Fit	Speech writing and presenting
Types of Resources	Links to information on various aspects of speech making
Authorship of Site	Diana Carlin and James Payne at the University of Kansas
Navigation	Good
Visual Appeal	Fair
Interactive Activity	None

The *Virtual Presentation Assistant* page can provide your students with many helpful links to sites and suggestions about speech making. Under the title, Researching Your Topic, for instance, are links to news resources, government and university libraries, and the *American Communication Reference Resources,* as well as advice on gathering information through interviews. Some of the other topics covered at this site are

■ Determining your purpose
■ Selecting your topic

- Analyzing your audience
- Supporting your points
- Outlining your points
- Using visual aids
- Presenting your speech
- Public speaking links

COMPOSING AND SHARING MUTIMEDIA PRESENTATIONS

Technology and Learning Website

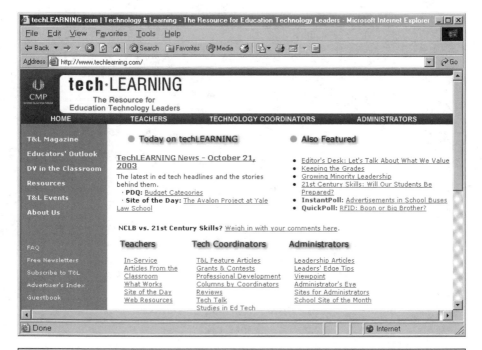

http://www.techlearning.com/	
Intended Audience	Teachers, technology directors, and administrators
Grade Level	K–12
Curricular Fit	Technological background information for educators
Types of Resources	Software reviews, school website building tools
Authorship of Site	Technology and Learning
Navigation	Good
Visual Appeal	Good
Interactive Activity	None

If you would like to construct a website for your class or school in order to establish projects with other schools, or to publish your students' writing assignments and multimedia Web projects on the Internet, then the home page produced by the editors of *Technology and Learning* magazine has much to offer. Reviews of more than 300 samples of English language arts software are available, as well as interviews with many leading experts on technology in schools. The following topics are explored in very informative hyperlinked articles about how to build your own website.

■ Why in the World Wide Web (Should We Build a Site of Our Own)?

■ Housing Your Site

■ Effective Site Design

■ GUI/RUI

■ Graphics

■ Spreading the Word

ENGLISH-AS-A-SECOND-LANGUAGE (ESL) PROJECTS AND RESOURCES

The Internet for ESL Teachers

http://edvista.com/claire/internet-esl.html	
Intended Audience	Teachers of ESL
Grade Level	All grades
Curricular Fit	ESL
Types of Resources	Many valuable links to ESL-related sites, teacher guidelines
Authorship of Site	Claire Bradin
Navigation	Good
Visual Appeal	Fair
Interactive Activity	MOOs, intercultural e-mail communication

From this page you can go to the Michigan State University ESL Student Project page to view some of the interesting projects that ESL students at MSU have produced, such as geographical reports, information about their experiences of culture shock, examples of their toughest grammar problems and solutions, and advice to new ESL students. Or you can enter a MOO for ESL students through the link to *schMOOze University,* which is a site on the Internet established in 1994 to provide people studying English as a second or foreign language with opportunities to practice English while they share ideas and experiences. Although *schMOOze University,* was originally intended for the use of ESL/EFL students, it welcomes all people interested in cross-cultural communication.

If you are interested in creating your own ESL web page, the *Internet for ESL Teachers* homepage provides, for example, a link to *Language Interactive,* a guide to web scripting for language learning. In its Dark Side of the Internet section, the *Internet for ESL Teachers* site introduces you to some of the more disturbing places that you should be aware of on the World Wide Web, such as the *School Sucks* site, where your students can download prewritten or customized essays instead of doing the writing themselves.

Linguistic Funland!

http://www.linguistic-funland.com/tesl-student-projects.html	
Intended Audience	Teachers and students of ESL
Grade Level	All grades
Curricular Fit	ESL
Types of Resources	Links to various worthwhile ESL project sites
Authorship of Site	Kristina Harris
Navigation	Good
Visual Appeal	Fair
Interactive Activity	ESL students can publish writing and read works by others

At *Linguistic Funland!* you and your students can find many interesting project ideas. Links are provided to sites about journal writing, English essays by Japanese students, a phrase pool, academic reading, and creative writing. Through the link to the *HUT International Writing Project* students can find writing topics such as taboos in specific cultures, how bilingualism affects people, and a memorable experience with a person from another culture.

Dave's ESL Cafe

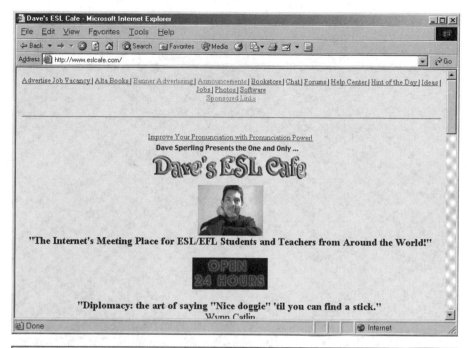

http://www.eslcafe.com/	
Intended Audience	Teachers and students of ESL
Grade Level	All grades
Curricular Fit	ESL
Types of Resources	Links to useful ESL sites
Authorship of Site	Dave Sperling
Navigation	Good
Visual Appeal	Good
Interactive Activity	ESL job listings around the globe, ESL chat rooms, and forums for teachers and students

At Dave Sperling's *ESL Cafe* there are links to a multitude of ESL job listings where you can look for ESL teaching opportunities for yourself around the globe. Or you can access ESL software and lesson plans to use with your students. This site also contains chat rooms and forums where your students can discuss the cinema, culture, family, food, etc. and where you can discuss with other ESL teachers activities and games, adult education, refugee issues, and much more. This is truly the best ESL site on the Internet, and is worth visiting even if you are not currently teaching ESL students.

INTERCULTURAL COMMUNICATION VIA E-MAIL

Voices of Youth

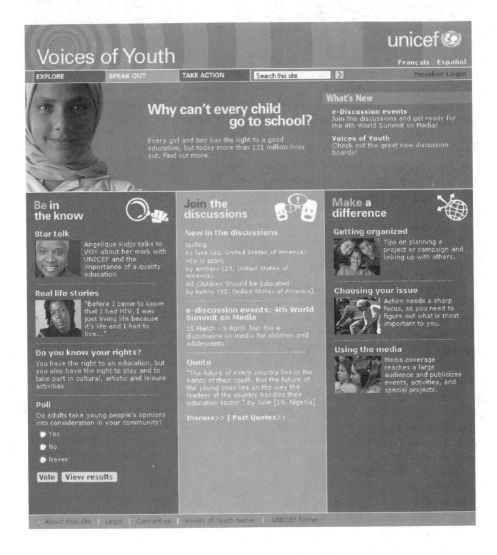

http://www.unicef.org/voy	
Intended Audience	Teachers and students
Grade Level	K–12
Curricular Fit	Reading and writing, intercultural communication, debate
Types of Resources	Classroom collaborative projects, teacher discussions
Authorship of Site	UNICEF
Navigation	Good
Visual Appeal	Good
Interactive Activity	Students can write to each other about human rights issues

In the *Voices of Youth* site children from around the world are encouraged by UNICEF to share with each other through live chats and e-mail messages their views about such global human rights issues such as child labor, HIV/AIDS, and children in war. One of the particularly ingenious multimedia interactive features of the site is the activity called The Whole Picture, in which students are shown a portion of a picture and asked to guess what the rest of the picture contains. In one picture, for instance, a boy is shown cringing while he looks away from the source of his fear. When the students click on the blank portion of the picture they see that the boy is in fact in a health clinic receiving a vaccination. The *Voices of Youth* site provides excellent opportunities for your students to learn about the issues important to their peers in other countries by talking to them directly about these issues.

ePALS Classroom Exchange

http://www.epals.com	
Intended Audience	Teachers and students
Grade Level	K–12
Curricular Fit	ESL, global issues theme units
Types of Resources	Lists of teachers and classes by subject, grade, and country
Authorship of Site	ePALS Classroom Exchange
Navigation	Good
Visual Appeal	Fair
Interactive Activity	E-mail intercultural exchanges

The *ePALS* site has linked more than 4.5 million students in 85,000 classrooms across 190 countries so that students can learn to express themselves across cultures by communicating with each other via the Internet. You can use the ePALS search engine to look for partners by country or city, classroom grade or age, or you can list your own school at the *ePALS* site and wait for another teacher to find you first. This is a wonderful and efficient way to connect your students to others around the globe.

The Electric Postcard

http://postcards.www.media.mit.edu/Postcards/Welcome.html	
Intended Audience	Teachers and students
Grade Level	K–12
Curricular Fit	Letter writing
Types of Resources	Various postcards that can be mailed electronically
Authorship of Site	Judith Donath at MIT Media Lab
Navigation	Good
Visual Appeal	Good
Interactive Activity	Choose your own postcards to post as email

Students can choose postcards to send by e-mail to their friends in other countries. These postcards can mark a holiday such as Hanukkah or Christmas, or they can highlight a certain artist's work such as Leonardo da Vinci or Paul Gauguin.

COMPARING OTHER LANGUAGES WITH ENGLISH

Conversational Mandarin Chinese Online

http://www.csulb.edu/~txie/ccol/content.htm	
Intended Audience	Teachers and students of languages
Grade Level	4–12
Curricular Fit	Chinese language within a multicultural literature theme unit
Types of Resources	Chinese phrases in audio files
Authorship of Site	Dr. Tianwei Xie
Navigation	Good
Visual Appeal	Fair
Interactive Activity	Choice of many audio clips

This is just one of hundreds of sites you could visit with your students in order to provide them with an introduction to a variety of foreign languages. The extensive lists of audio clips available at this particular site are organized under the following categories: greetings, shopping, dining, traveling, and time.

CREATING SCHOOL HOMEPAGES

Banksia Secondary College Homepage

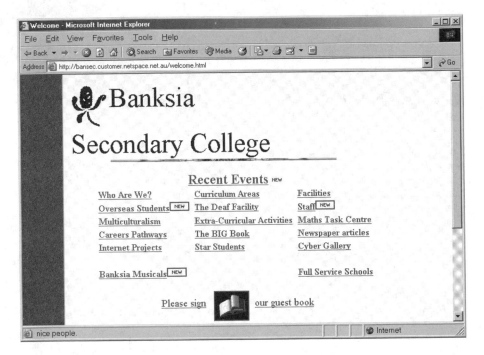

http://bansec.customer.netspace.net.au/welcome.html	
Intended Audience	Teachers and students
Grade Level	8–12
Curricular Fit	Creative writing and intercultural communication
Types of Resources	Art, short stories, student biographies
Authorship of Site	Banksia School
Navigation	Good
Visual Appeal	Good
Interactive Activity	Travel with students on field trip, read creative writing

One way that you can help to make your school's presence known on the Internet is to develop a school home page that contains imaginative images and writing from your students. The *Banksia Secondary College Home Page* in Australia contains many interesting features that reflect the multicultural composition of the school. In a section titled the Banksia Big Book Archives, visiting students can read some of the best stories written each year by students from various grade levels in the school. In a letter to a racist Australian politician, for example, a Somalian refugee student states,

"Who do you think you are? Does Australian politics allow this sort of behavior in our country? Personally, I don't like racism, but you seem to be enjoying your new job promoting it." In another piece an Indonesian boy describes his escape from an erupting volcano before he moved to Australia. "Flaming boulders had tossed across the horizons and dropped down killing people before they had a chance to find shelter. The army couldn't help the survivors, because the black ashes covered the main road and made it very difficult for them to get into the remote areas. Few survived the disaster, I was one of them."

Some other imaginative ways in which Banksia's teachers use its home page to establish their students' identities on the Internet are to (1) exhibit their students' artwork in a Cyber Gallery; (2) highlight in a "Star Students" item the accomplishments and cultural backgrounds of their immigrant students from Somalia, Vietnam, Lebanon, China, the Philippines, Indonesia, Ethiopia, and sixteen other countries; (3) present photographic essays about school life such as the one in which the grade 7, 8, and 9 ESL students are shown making an excursion to a nearby wildlife sanctuary; and (4) describe in their Cyber News articles events such as the visit to their school of the Mayi Winba Dancers, an Aboriginal troupe from Northern Queensland.

International WWW School Registry

http://www.grandpajunior.com/School-list.shtml	
Intended Audience	Teachers and students
Grade Level	K–12
Curricular Fit	Publishing home pages on the Internet
Types of Resources	Global list of elementary and secondary school home pages
Authorship of Site	Grandpa Junior—Webmaster
Navigation	Good
Visual Appeal	Good
Interactive Activity	Vast collection of links to schools worldwide

If you want to visit a number of school homepages in order to make connections with other teachers or to consider ways of making your own school's homepage more interesting, you can use Grandpa Junior's *International WWW School Web Site Registry,* which contains the homepages of thousands of schools around the world. Many of the middle and secondary school homepages that you can discover through this site contain information about each school's students and teachers such as their own individual homepages and e-mail addresses. Once you have found a school whose teachers and students might prove interesting partners for collaborative responses to world literature or cultural exchanges, you can send an e-mail to the teachers you have chosen and plan together possible activities between your classes.

NEWSPAPERS AND MAGAZINES
The Media Literacy Online Project

http://interact.uoregon.edu/MediaLit/HomePage	
Intended Audience	Teachers and students
Grade Level	6–12
Curricular Fit	Media literacy
Types of Resources	Research into children and the media, media course syllabi, media guides, etc.
Authorship of Site	College of Education, University of Oregon
Navigation	Good
Visual Appeal	Fair
Interactive Activity	None

The goal of the *Media Literacy Online Project* is to provide a support service for teachers, and others, concerned with the influence of media in the lives of children and youth. The site's authors have created this comprehensive media literacy resource collection to facilitate that objective. This extensive set of resources includes among its many links research into children and the media, media course syllabi, media guides (such as the PBS Teacher Resource), media museums, media production by and for children and youth, censorship, advertising, media violence, and online newspaper, magazine, music, radio, film and television services.

The Globe and Mail

Reprinted with permission from *The Globe and Mail*

http://www.theglobeandmail.com/index.html	
Intended Audience	Teachers and students
Grade Level	6–12
Curricular Fit	Newspapers in the classroom
Types of Resources	National and international news stories
Authorship of Site	The Globe and Mail
Navigation	Good
Visual Appeal	Good
Interactive Activity	None

The Globe and Mail is just one of hundreds of newspapers and magazines from around the world that are available via the Internet. Students can use newspaper sites such as these as models for their own newspaper writing activities; they can base their creative writing on the current events which they see recorded in these online newspapers; or they can sample a number of these papers from various countries to compare the opinions they express about international stories. At *The Globe and Mail* site, for instance, they can read international and national news stories, business, sports, arts, and recreation items.

Adbusters Online Magazine

http://adbusters.org/home/	
Intended Audience	Teachers and students
Grade Level	9–12
Curricular Fit	Media studies and journalism
Types of Resources	Magazine articles, advertising spoofs
Authorship of Site	AdBusters Media Foundation
Navigation	Good
Visual Appeal	Good
Interactive Activity	Responding to and writing radical ads

This site contains many excellent advertising spoofs and articles that help students to develop critical media literacy. It is intended for students who are in high school or university. Back issues of the electronic version of the magazine are available at this site for free. Students may also wish to contribute their own writing and artwork to the annual, juried International Festival of Radical Communication.

SUGGESTED ACTIVITIES

1. Encourage your students to visit the *Luminarium* site, where each of them can study a different medieval or Renaissance writer. In their reports to the class they can consider imaginative ways to bring their author's work to life. While reading from Chaucer, for instance, they can learn from the audio clips at the site how to pronounce Middle English and then read aloud to their classmates using the appropriate pronunciation. Or they can display images of original illuminated manuscripts.

2. As part of a writer's workshop in which you are encouraging students to edit each other's work and to concentrate upon improving grammatical expression, show them the *Guide to Grammar and Writing* website where they can learn how to correct basic sentence errors, usage errors, etc.

3. After visiting *The Eclectic Writer* and *The Write Site* with your students, have them try their hand at crime writing, mystery writing, newspaper feature story writing, screen writing, etc. Then have them publish the resulting texts in their own online school newspaper or magazine.

4. Have each of your students read a different speech from the writings of famous women at the *Gifts of Speech* site. Then encourage them to write speeches of their own in response to the ones that they have read. To guide your students' speech writing, introduce them to the information at the *Virtual Presentation Assistant* site on effective speech writing and delivery.

5. Ask your students to study the information at the *Technology and Learning Website,* and then help them to work together in teams to create multimedia web projects on themes related to your regular course work.

6. Take your students to the three ESL homepages presented in this chapter, and help them to listen to radio programs or to take part in a language listening lab.

7. Take your students to UNICEF's *Voices of Youth* site and involve them in a live chat or email conference with children around the world on a human rights issue such as child labor. Or, through the Epals Classroom Exchange site, connect your whole class with students in a class in another part of the world to carry out a cooperative project based upon the issues raised at UNICEF's site.

8. Involve your students in visiting several school homepages via the *International WWW School Registry,* then have them create or revise your school's homepage.

SUMMARY

We have argued throughout this book that developments in technology have obliged teachers to consider a new paradigm for the teaching of language arts. In this final chapter we have made use of the NCTE Standards for the English language arts to organize our presentation of sites and activities. We have indicated, for instance, that, if your goal is to develop in your students "an understanding and respect for diversity," you can accomplish this now by enabling your students to carry out intercultural communication via e-mail with the help of sites such as *ePALS* and UNICEF's *Voices of Youth.* Or if your goal is to help your students to "read literature from many periods," then the *Luminarium* site can be employed to bring the works of writers such as Chaucer to life through media formats and archives that were not available to language arts teachers even five years ago. We wish you many enjoyable hours of reading and writing adventures as you extend the range and variety of literacy activities that your students can experience, thanks to the communicative power of the Internet. We hope that the new vision of English teaching you thus embrace will excite you and your students for years to come.

GLOSSARY

An Internet Language for Easy Browsing

The Internet has its own special language. An understanding of this language is an asset for easy browsing and communicating.

American Standard Code for Information Interchange (ASCII) is a format recognized by the computer as containing text and numbers and no graphics.

Attached files are files that are attached to e-mail and that can therefore be sent from one computer to another. This includes audio files, video clips, and images such as photographs.

Bandwidth, in bits per second, is a measure of how much data a modem transfers from one end to another.

Baud rate tells how many bits per second a modem can receive or send data. It is the measure of speed of the modem. Bandwith is the measure of quantity. For example, a 2,400 baud modem transfers over 9,600 bits per second of data.

Bit is a number that the computer uses, either one or zero, to translate and understand data. It is the smallest unit of measurement in computer data.

Browser is software used to view and extract resources from home pages and web pages on the Internet. The popular browser programs are Netscape and Microsoft Internet Explorer.

Bulletin Board System (BBS) is an online "get-together" system for people to share resources and ideas. A BBS is hosted by an individual or a society.

Byte is made up of eight bits. A kilobyte is 1,024 bytes. A small diskette carries about 1.33 kilobytes.

CD (compact disk) is a metal disk that can carry 700 megabytes of information. Most computers now have the capability to save or burn information onto CDs. Some CDs are rewriteable so that you can save information on them more than once.

Common Gateway Interface (CGI) is script-based software, usually written by programmers in Practical Extraction and Report Language (PERL), to instruct the web server to carry out certain operations. CGI programs/scripts are usually put into a directory called cgi-bin.

Cyberspace, a term coined by William Gibson, describes the world of the Internet that carries a huge amount of informational resources through computer networks.

Domain, also known as *DNS (Domain Name System)*, personalizes every computer in the world on the Internet. It gives a computer a number or word identification (**www.altavista.com**, for example, is a unique DNS). No two people have the same DNS.

Electronic-mail (e-mail) is a software tool that is used on the Internet to send text across the Internet from one computer to another simultaneously.

Frequently Asked Questions (FAQs) are found on many websites. The FAQ page is a place where people can look up answers to related questions on a particular subject of interest. You can get FAQs on the Internet through personal or commercial web pages. Many of the author sites in this book contain FAQ pages.

Graphics Interchange Format (GIF) is graphic file formatted into GIF classification. Many Internet graphics files are in this GIF format. Another popular graphic format is *jpg*, which is a compressed graphic file.

Homepage is an Internet site reached by an Internet browser. An Internet site starting with **http://** protocol is called a *homepage* or a *website*.

Host is a computer that provides other computers on the Internet with a variety of services such as homepage storage or just printing.

Hypertext is text that can be linked to other documents by the click of a mouse. Hypertexts are underlined in blue.

HyperText Markup Language (HTML) refers to computer scripting language. It is used to make web pages or homepages. HTML documents can usually be recognized by their *htm* or *html* extensions. HTML is used to format and lay out a web page.

HyperText Transport Protocol (HTTP) is used on the Internet to locate hypertext information-based files. Sites with the HTTP protocol are World Wide Web sites.

Inter-Connected-Network (Internet) is a network of computers that share informational resources. Thousands of computers around the world are linked through the Internet to provide and share resource materials.

Internet Protocol Number (IP number) is a number used to identify your computer on the Internet. An IP number on the Internet is equivalent to a social security number.

Internet Relay Chat (IRC) is an online live chat environment on the Internet. IRC provides opportunities to communicate and conference with colleagues and friends.

Internet Service Provider (ISP) is an organization that provides access to the Internet for a price.

Intranet is a private, local information-based network, the opposite of the Internet. No "outsider" can retrieve data from this network. The network resources are available only to members of the organization.

Listserv is a mailing list that belongs to a group of people with the same interest. Members can share ideas via e-mail.

Local Area Network (LAN) is limited to a specific site or building.

Login is the term used to describe how you are to enter a website that requires membership. Usually after you type in your username you are then required as well to type in a password to gain full access to the site.

Multipurpose Internet Mail Extension (MIME) is used as a standard to include non-ASCII files with e-mail messages. Examples of non-ASCII files are sound, movie, and graphic files.

Newsgroup is a service provider for Internet discussions via e-mail. You can post messages on a "news" computer system.

Point-to-Point Protocol (PPP) enables a computer to initiate a normal connection (*TCP/IP*) through a modem and a telephone line to connect to the Internet.

Router is a computer hardware device used to connect two or more networks together.

Server is a computer or software package that initiates and relays all sorts of computer services to network client computers or client software.

Slip stands for *Serial Line Internet Protocol*. It is similar to PPP.

Uniform Resource Locator (URL) is the standard syntax to locate any resource available on the Internet. It is the equivalent of an address for a website. An example of a URL is **http://www.stfx.ca.**

UNIX is a computer operating system for SUN computers. It is a multiuser computer operating system (DOS and MacOS are examples of simpler computer operating systems).

World Wide Web (WWW) is a subset of the Internet.